H.O.P.E.

Holding Onto Positive Expectations

A Spiritual Journey Towards An Empowering Transformed Life

Facilitator's Guide
Workbook and Journal Included

Written by
Andrea J. Williams M.S.

AuthorHouse™
1663 Liberty Drive, Suite 200
Bloomington, IN 47403
www.authorhouse.com
Phone: 1-800-839-8640

First published by AuthorHouse 5/6/2009
ISBN: 978-1-4389-2270-6 (sc)

Printed in the United States of America
Bloomington, Indiana

This book is printed on acid-free paper.

Scripture quotations are taken from the Holy Bible, New Living Translation, copyright © 1996. Used by permission of Tyndale House Publishers, Inc., Wheaton, Illinois 60189. All rights reserved.

Scriptures taken from the New King James Version. Copyright © 1979, 1980, 1982 by Thomas Nelson, Inc. Used by permission. All rights reserved.

authorHOUSE®

Contents

History and Purpose   1

Curriculum Description   2
    Module I   2
    The Mind   2
    Module II   2
    The Body   2
    Module III   2
    The Spirit   2

Introductory Meeting   6

Lesson I   7
    What Type of Soil Is Your Mind?   7

Lesson II   8
    Tilling the Soil: Plowing and Harrowing   8

Lesson III   9
    Tilling the Soil: Fertilization   9

Lesson IV   11
    Tending the Garden   11

*Lesson V   15
    Relationships   15

Lesson VI   17
    Personal Growth   17

Lesson VII   18
    Life Success   18

Lesson VIII   19
    Health   19

Lesson IX   22
    Declaring Your Mission Statement   22

*Lesson X   23
    Organizational Structure   23

*Lesson XI   26
    Standard Operating Procedures   26

Lesson XII   28
    Quality Assurance   28

Preface   30

Garden of H.O.P.E.   34

Your Journey begins…   34

Lesson I   41
   What Type of Soil Is Your Mind?   41

Lesson II   43
   Tilling the Soil: Plowing and Harrowing   43

Lesson III   46

Lesson IV   48
   Tending the Garden   48

Lesson II   111
   Tilling the Soil: Plowing and Harrowing   111

Lesson III   115
   Tilling the Soil: Fertilization   115

Lesson IV   117
   Tending the Garden   117

Lesson V   126
   Relationships   126

Lesson VI   129
   Personal Growth   129
   Actualization of Gifts and Talents   129

Week VII   140
   Life Success   140

Lesson VII   141
   Life Success   141

Lesson VIII   143
   Health   143

Lesson IX   154
   Declaring Your Mission Statement   154

Lesson X   157
   Organizational Structure   157

Lesson XI   160
   Standard Operating Procedures   160

Lesson XI   162
   Standard Operating Procedures   162

Lesson XII   164
   Quality Assurance   164

About the Author   167

History and Purpose

This workbook is first and foremost an assignment from the Lord. In 2001, the Lord placed me in an environment where I served a population of people who for the most part presented as *hopeless*. As a result of this experience, I felt a strong compulsion to do something, because at a point and time in my life, I too was *very* hopeless. Fortunately, with the Lord's hand over my life, He led and guided me along a path where I was able to move beyond a life of hopelessness to a life of *complete* joy, hope, and fruitfulness. I wanted the same for the population I served. I was determined to work towards bridging the gap between the abyss of hopelessness, and the realization of attaining and living a fruitful and hopeful life.

Armed with this determination, various data gathering tools and intervention techniques, I was able to probe more into the root cause of this deep-seated feeling of hopelessness. I soon realized the problem stemmed from any one, or a combination of the following situations:

- Childhood trauma, or a traumatic event that was never resolved, and as a result the individual set out on his or her life's journey with a defeatist posture.
- An on-going losing battle with substance abuse and/or mental illness.
- A series of setbacks and disappointing events that seem to have crippled the individual's ability to think rationally, and act responsibly.
- A perpetuation of generational woes or curses.
- A decline in one's morals, values, and spirituality as a result of living a "lie" and/or a reprehensible lifestyle.

Using the information gathered, I, in conjunction with the guidance and grace of the Holy Spirit created this work of **excellence**. I *strongly* believe the lessons and activities presented in this workbook will help those who are living life in a state of perpetual *hopelessness,* move away from their present state of being to a life that is ***spiritually transformed and empowered.***

I am not claiming to have the answers to all of life's problems, nor am I negating the valuable services of substance abuse and mental health counseling, Christian counseling preferably, if and when needed. However, I do believe "true" life-long change in one's life can *only* be achieved through the combination of **Divine Intervention**, and a sincere desire on one's behalf to wholeheartedly commit to, and embrace the process of change by faith and Spirit-led effort.

Curriculum Description

H.O.P.E. (Holding Onto Positive Expectations), is a faith-based curriculum that focuses on one's ability to realize a spiritually empowered transformed life through maximizing one's potential based upon the principle of *sowing and harvesting*. The seeds **sown** are the expectations the participant has for his or her spiritually empowered transformed life, and that which is manifested from the expectations is the **harvest**.

Another tenet that provides for the underpinning of this curriculum is the idea of *holism*. This holistic approach encompasses the components of mind, body, and spirit. In order for an individual to successfully achieve his or her endeavor towards a spiritually empowered transformed life, there must be a distinct degree of *connectedness* and *synergy* between these three components.

This twelve weeks curriculum is divided into three modules (See Fig. I); an explanation of the modules is as follows:

Module I
The Mind

In this module, the ***mind*** is likened to a garden, and is described as the participant's Garden of HOPE. Based upon the parable of the **Four Soils** in Matthew 13, the participant explores the condition of his or her mind, and identifies the type of mind soil that exists in his or her garden. Upon completion of this exploration, the participant then undergoes the process of preparing his or her garden through the tilling process, and eventually plants the seeds of positive expectation in his or her garden.

Module II
The Body

In this module, the participant is introduced to the concepts of *stewardship* and *wholeness* as each one relates to *spiritual*/body intactness. From the perspective of a steward, the participant will explore spiritual *wholeness* in the areas of relationship, personal growth, life success, and health.

Module III
The Spirit

Upon completing this module, the participant will be spiritually grounded. In this module, the *life* of the participant is likened to a *business*. By declaring a spiritual mission statement for his or her business, the participant will identify his or her spiritual purpose.

The participant will also examine the organizational structure within the business, establish standard operating procedures for the business, discover his or her primary duties and responsibilities in the business, and assess the efficacy of his or her business.

Uses of Curriculum

This curriculum is ideal for correctional settings, churches, and any faith-based organization in the community purposing to meet the needs of those who are *hopeless* and *spiritually* lost.

The Workbook

The accompanying workbook is ideal for *group* settings, as well as self-directed individual use. In a group setting, it is at the facilitator's discretion when the group convenes for meetings. I strongly recommend having an initial introductory meeting before meeting for the first lesson. This meeting will serve several purposes. As the facilitator it is recommended that you use this meeting to establish your guidelines, rules, procedures, and expectations for the upcoming weeks. This initial meeting should also be used to establish your group cohesiveness. I also recommend that the group meets at least two to three times per week each lesson. Note; there will be times when the group needs to meet *every* night per week, as some lessons encompass more exercises, and are lengthier than others, an asterisk (*) will denote those lessons. It is also at the facilitator's discretion to have participants work through the lessons prior to group meetings or during each group meeting.

Delivery of Modules

Module I Weeks 1-4 The Mind	Module II Weeks 5-8 The Body	Module III Weeks 9-12 The Spirit
Week I **Lesson I** What Type of Soil Is Your Mind?	**Week V** **Lesson V** Relationships	**Week IX** **Lesson IX** Declaring Your Mission Statement
Week II **Lesson II** Tilling the Soil: Plowing and Harrowing	**Week VI** **Lesson VI** Personal Growth	**Week X** **Lesson X** Organizational Structure
Week III **Lesson III** Tilling the Soil: Fertilization	**Week VII** **Lesson VII** Life Success	**Week XI** **Lesson XI** Standard Operating Procedures
Week IV **Lesson IV** Tending the Garden	**Week VIII** **Lesson VIII** Health	**Week XII** **Lesson XII** Quality Assurance

Fig. 1

Part One

Lessons 1 to 4

THE MIND

"…But we can understand these things, for we have the mind of Christ."

1 Corinthians 2:16

Andrea J. Williams M.S.

Introductory Meeting

Objective: To establish group setting, guidelines, and cohesiveness.

Tools Needed: Workbook, Bible, Pencils or Pens

- Begin the meeting in prayer asking for God's direction and guidance; explain that all meetings will begin in prayer.

- Introduce yourself to group members and have the members introduce themselves to each other.

- Have participants review the introduction of the workbook, ask the group members if anyone of them have asked any of the questions posed in the introduction. Illuminate commonality of responses to generate the feeling of **cohesiveness**.

- Discuss the importance of having a synergistic relationship between the mind, body, and spirit in the process of transformation. Review the major points that will be discussed and explored in each section of the workbook.

- Discuss "Your Journey Begins….." Read **Genesis 2:8** as a group, and then ask the question, "Why do you think God created a garden to place the first man He created in?" After receiving a few responses state to the group, "God knows that a garden was and continues to be a great place for **New Beginnings;** and the journey each one of you is about to embark upon is all about New Beginnings."

- Finally, have those participants who are willing share some of the expectations they have for their new spiritually empowered, transformed life.

- Before ending this session, reiterate to the group members the importance of each one of them understanding and abiding by the group's rules, procedures, and expectations.

- End this meeting in prayer of thanksgiving and ask for God's direction, grace, and guidance for the upcoming weeks.

Lesson I

Week I

What Type of Soil Is Your Mind?
A Closer Examination

Objective: To emphasize that a changed life first begins in a changed mind.

Tools Needed: Workbook, Bible, Pencils or Pens

- Begin the session with prayer, ask the Holy Spirit to lead and guide you and the group members into **all** truths.

- Read Romans 12:2, emphasize that a changed life first begins in the mind. Ask the group members, "Why is it that satan attacks the mind?" Discuss the responses. Ask for participants to volunteer personal experiences about how they have been attacked in their minds, and the events that followed after the attacks.

- Read the Parable of the Four Soils in Matthew 13:3-8 and 18-23. Ask several participants to share his or her summary of the parable. Discuss the parable with the group members. Of the four soil types in the parable, have the group members identify the infertile and fertile mediums, and the characteristics of the fertile medium verses that of the infertile ones.

- Tell the participants that their minds are a medium, and have them share their responses to questions #1 and #2 of lesson one.

- Discuss with the group members the need to create a fertile environment in their minds, as they will be planting their seeds of expectation there. Emphasize to the group members that their mind is their **GARDEN OF H.O.P.E.** Have them identify the spiritual importance of this task.

- End the session with prayer, thanking the Holy Spirit for His guidance.

Lesson II
Week II

Tilling the Soil: Plowing and Harrowing

Objective: To create a fertile environment in the mind.

Tools Needed: Workbook, Bible, Pencils or Pens

- Begin the session with prayer, ask the Holy Spirit to lead and guide you and the group members into **all** truths.

- Introduce and discuss the tilling process with the group members.

- Review the plowing exercise with the members. This exercise could have been challenging for some of the members, as it required each member to first identify all those things in their lives that have contaminated their mind soil. Secondly, each member needed to loosen and disconnect themselves from those contaminants. Remember, for many of the group members, these contaminants were a part of their world and experiences for a very long time; therefore, allow for, and encourage discussions.

- Review the harrowing journal exercise. Again, this exercise might have been challenging for some of the members. Allow for, and encourage discussions.

- Before ending this session, **emphasize** the importance of thoroughly completing both the plowing and harrowing exercises before moving onto lesson three in the workbook. Remind the group members that they are in the process of **creating a fertile environment in their minds.**

- End the session in prayer, thanking the Holy Spirit for His guidance.

Lesson III

Week III

Tilling the Soil: Fertilization

Objective: To create a fertile environment in the mind.

Tools Needed: Workbook, Bible, Pencils or Pens, CD or Tape Player, Relaxation Music

- Begin the session with prayer, ask the Holy Spirit to lead and guide you and the group members into **all** truths.

- It is most imperative that you conduct this session with group members who have thoroughly completed the plowing and harrowing process.

- Complete the guided imagery exercise below with the group members. Guide them through this exercise again; even though, they have completed it in their workbooks individually, through the group approach it will evoke a different experience.

- Guided Imagery exercise: Begin the music, say to the participants:

"Close your eyes and take a deep breath, hold it for a second, release it, take another deep breath, hold it for a second, release it. With your eyes still closed, listen."

Read the imagery exercised below. When you have reached the end, **tell the group members to keep their eyes closed for about one to two seconds, then, have them open their eyes.**

Visualize your Garden of H.O.P.E. plowed and harrowed. As you walk throughout your garden barefooted, feel the soil beneath your feet and between your toes. Walk down each row slowly spreading the fertilizer as you go, appreciate the fertile medium you have created in your mind with the help of the Holy Spirit. When you have reached the end of the last row, STOP. Stoop down and pick up a handful of soil, look at how loose, contaminant-free, and enriched it appears. Now allow the soil to fall back to the ground through your fingers. Visualize the harvest you are expecting, see how lush; green, and bountiful it appears. Now say to yourself, "By faith, I believe and receive this harvest, in Jesus' Name. Amen."

- Have group members share their experience with this imagery exercise. Then, have those participants, who are willing, share some of their seeds of expectations they have planted in their **Garden of H.O.P.E.**
- End this session by reading Matthew 21:22, Psalms 37:4-5, and a prayer of encouragement.

Lesson IV

Week IV

Tending the Garden

Objective: To emphasize the importance of maintaining a fertile medium.

Tools Needed: Workbook, Bible, Pencils or Pens

- Begin the session with prayer, ask the Holy Spirit to lead and guide you and the group members into **all** truths.

- Ask the group members the following question, "If you wanted your garden to thrive, how would you go about tending it?" Key words to note in the responses received are **watering**, **fertilizing**, **weeding**, and protecting or **safeguarding** from intruders.

- Have the group members turn to Philippians 4:6-7 in their Bibles, and read as a group. Review in the workbook the indications of watering too much or too little.

- Discuss the importance of pulling the weeds of anxiety, fear, doubt, self-pity, impatience, laziness, insecurity, lack of self-confidence, worry, poor self-esteem/worth, guilt, and shame from the garden. Have group members identify other types of weeds that might choke the life out of their garden.

- Discuss **spiritual maturation** and **spiritual stagnation**. Ask the group members to provide behaviors related to spiritual maturation and spiritual stagnation. Talk about the importance of growth in their spiritual walk with the Lord. Stress to the group members that regular fertilizing is vital for proper growth. Have the members give examples of providing fertilizer to their garden. Responses will vary, but should include any of the following: reading the Bible, attending a good Bible teaching church regularly, and living a holy and righteous life.

- Ask the group members, "On a scale of **1-10**, with **10** being the greatest, how much do you value the opinions of others about you, and your life?" Talk about the dangers of valuing the opinions of others, especially during this journey of transformation.

- Review the journal exercise, **"How Well Are You Tending Your Garden?"** with the group members; encourage them to tend to their garden regularly. As the weeks progress, check on the group members' progress in this exercise.

- End this session with prayer, thanking the Holy Spirit for His guidance.

Part Two

Lessons 5 to 8

THE BODY

"You made all the delicate, inner parts of my body and knit me together in my mother's womb. Thank you for making me so wonderfully complex! Your workmanship is marvelous…"

Psalm 139: 13-14

As the lessons in this section are based on the concepts of ***stewardship*** and ***wholeness***, it is recommended that time is spent thoroughly discussing and exploring these two concepts from the biblical perspective ***before*** moving onto lesson four.

Stewardship

After reviewing the definition of *steward*, read the scripture **I Corinthians 6:19-20**, reiterate to group members the *fact* that their bodies **do not** belong to them. Their bodies belong to God, the Creator of life! Have group members share their reaction to the revelation that their body does not belong to them.

Wholeness

First, have group members give their definition or perception of *wholeness*, then, review the two perspectives on wholeness from the workbook. Read John 15:5, 7-8. Ask the group members if they believe this scripture reflects a *true* meaning of wholeness. Have members share their responses about how the two perspectives on wholeness differ.

NOTE: In this section of the workbook, the groups will need to meet *every* night of the week to thoroughly process and complete each lesson.

*Lesson V

Week V

Relationships

Objective: To understand the importance of relationships in our lives; first, with Jesus Christ, secondly, with the "self," and thirdly with others.

Tools Needed: Workbook, Bible, Pencils or Pens

- Begin the session with prayer, ask the Holy Spirit to lead and guide you and the group members into **all** truths.

- Read Genesis 2:18 as a group. Have the group members discuss why relationships are important.

- Ask the group members **"What is the most important relationship in your life?"** After you have received a few responses, state that the **most** important relationship in all our lives is the one we have or should have with Jesus Christ. Read John 15:5-8. Discuss this scripture by keying in on **John 15:8**. **Emphasize** to the group members that a true disciple is the one who produces much fruit, and in order to be a true disciple, **you have to be a born-again believer.** Ask group members for a show of hand of those who do not understand what being "born-again" means, and explain to the whole group the meaning, importance, and significance of **salvation**. Go over the sinner's prayer that is in the workbook. State to the group members that it is pointless to move on in this workbook by faith, if there is **no** relationship with Jesus Christ. Extend an invitation to those members of the group who would like to receive the free gift of salvation, or re-dedicate their lives to Christ.

- Emphasize to the group members that establishing or re-establishing a relationship with the "self" is not about self-centeredness, but about the exploration and validation of the "true" self. Have the members share their responses to the exercise: **Describe the type of relationship that exists between you and your "self." Would you say that it is (1) Nonexistent, (2) Casual, or (3) Intimate?**

- Focus on the importance of re-establishing or establishing a relationship with the "self".

Discuss the three steps involved in this process. In **Step I**, relationship types and roles of the "self" are explored. It is important for members of the group to identify all the relationship types and roles their "self" occupies and functions in. In **Step II**, have group members share the expectations and demands placed upon each role he or she is required to meet, then, have them share the expectations and demands that he or she is **only** capable of truly satisfying.

- In **Step III**, the group members will complete the task of establishing or re-establishing a relationship with their "true self." Discuss the "Self Wheel," (Fig. A and Fig. B) and all of its components.

- As you begin the "Discovering the True Self" discussion, reiterate the importance of walking in the "true" self. Review all the exercises included in this section. **A**. Identifying Your Strengths and Limitations, **B**. Identifying Your Beliefs and Values, and **C**. Defining Your "true" Self, with the group participants. Have volunteers share their "True" Self Wheel and journal exercise, "True" Self essay with other members in the group.

- End this session in prayer, thanking the Holy Spirit for His guidance.

Lesson VI
Week VI

Personal Growth

Objective: To emphasize that "personal growth" is a mandate given to a *steward,* and the task of personal growth is accomplished through a *sound* character.

Tools Needed: Workbook, Bible, Pens or Pencils.

- Begin the session with prayer, ask the Holy Spirit to lead and guide you and the group members into **all** truths.

- Discuss with the group members the difference between a positive, productive life, and a life that is stagnant. Ask them to give three attributes of a positive, productive life, and three attributes of a stagnant life.

- Review and discuss the definitions for **talents** and **gifts**.

- Have the group participants share their responses to the five sentences about gifts and talents in the workbook.

- As a group, read **Proverbs 11:3** and **Galatians 5:22-23**. Ask the group members, "What is a sound character?" Emphasize to the group members the importance of possessing a sound character, and that the main attributes of a sound character are integrity, and the gifts of the fruit of the Spirit, as mentioned in Galatians 5:22-23._

- Review the **"Character Building"** exercise with the group. Have the participants begin the exercise immediately. Review the participants' progress periodically throughout the upcoming weeks.

- Re-visit the "How Well Are You Tending Your Garden?" exercise. Have each group participant give a report about his or her progress.

- End the session in prayer, thanking the Holy Spirit for His guidance.

Lesson VII
Week VII

Life Success

Objective: To emphasis that a *truly* successful life lies within words spoken and the attitude of the heart.

Tools Needed: Workbook, Bible, Pens or Pencils.

- Begin the session with prayer, ask the Holy Spirit to lead and guide you and the group members into **all** truths.

- As a group review the section in the workbook that discusses the consistency between Psalms 1:3,6, and the dictionary's definition of success. Reiterate to the group participants that a life of true success is one that **honors** and **glorifies** God, and is anchored to **words** spoken and the **attitude** of the heart.

- Ask the group participants the following questions; (1) How have your words hurt your life and the lives of others? (2) How have the words of others hurt your life? (3) How have your words nourished your life and the lives of others? (4) How have the words of others nourished your life?

- Review the **Common Situation** exercise. Have participants share some of their responses from their journals.

- As a group read Jeremiah 17:9-10 and Matthew 15:19. Discuss the seriousness of these two scriptures and the need to engage in consistent heart attitude examinations. Review the related journal exercise, "The Attitude of the Heart."

- Review the participants' progress with the **Character Building** exercise. Have each participant give a report about his or her progress.

- End the session in prayer, thanking the Holy Spirit for His guidance.

Lesson VIII

Week VIII

Health

Objective: To promote a healthy perspective about life by emphasizing the importance of releasing the weight of past hurts and pain, and the heaviness of guilt and shame.

Tools Needed: Workbook, Bible, Pens, and Pencils

- Begin the session in prayer, ask the Holy Spirit to lead you and the group members into **all** truths.

- Discuss the affects of long-term weight gain in the physical body, and the preventative measures that should be taken to promote good physical health. Using the same example of weight gain in the physical body, have the group members discuss the adverse affects past hurts, pain, guilt, and shame can have upon the body, mind, and spirit if left unattended and unresolved.

- Review the **Releasing IT** exercise with the participants. Encourage discussion and feedback as you go through the review. **Stress** the importance of completing this exercise.

- Revisit the "How Well Are You Tending Your Garden?" exercise. Have each group member give a report about his or her progress.

- End the session in prayer, thanking the Holy Spirit for His guidance.

Part Three

Lesson 9 to 12

THE SPIRIT

"…I have been crucified with Christ. I myself no longer live, but Christ lives in me. So I live my life in this earthly body by trusting in the Son of God, who loved me and gave himself for me."
Galatians 2:19-20

Lesson IX
Week IX

Declaring Your Mission Statement

Objective: To affirm your spiritual purpose through the declaration of your mission statement.

Tools Needed: Workbook, Bible, Pens, and Pencils

- Begin the session in prayer, ask the Holy Spirit to lead you and the group members into **all** truths.

- Review the meaning of a steward from part two of the workbook. Remind the participants that they are all stewards of the life (their business) that was given to them by God, **but** God is the **owner** of their lives, their business.

- Discuss in detail the meaning of the "Spirit man." Read and discuss **Genesis 1:27** and **John 4:24**; explain to the participants that they are created in the image of God, and God is a Spirit. Reiterate to the participants that the only way the steward is legally able to establish his or her business is through having a personal on-going relationship with the Godhead; the Father, Son, and Holy Spirit. Once this relationship is established, then a spiritual purpose must be identified and a mission statement declared.

- Review and discuss with the participants the "Declaring Your Mission Statement" journal exercise. Have the participants share their thoughts, and for those who are willing, share their mission statements with others in the group.

- End the session in prayer, thanking the Holy Spirit for His guidance.

*Lesson X

Week X

Organizational Structure

Objective: To understand the hierarchal order and the flow of the chain-of-command within your business.

Tools Needed: Workbook, Bible, Pens, and Pencils

- Begin the session in prayer, ask the Holy Spirit to lead you and the group members into **all** truths.

- Discuss with the participants the meaning of hierarchy, "A body of persons organized or classified according to rank, capacity, or authority." The American Heritage Dictionary of the English Language. Explain to the participants that their business is a partnership (a body of persons) between the Owner/Head, spirit man, and the steward. Therefore, based on the meaning of hierarchy, it is most important that a hierarchical order is established within the business.

- Continue with the discussion of hierarchical order by addressing how the body of persons is classified within the business;

1. The Owner/Head is the **Trinity**, and is positioned at the top of the hierarchical order. Review the components and nature of the Head as it is explained in the workbook.
2. The **spirit man** follows the Trinity in the hierarchical order. Stress the importance of the spiritual connection between the spirit man and the Trinity, and the need for there to be an ongoing personal relationship.
3. The steward follows the spirit man. Reiterate that it is the steward's responsibility to maintain the integrity and order of the business as it apply to the "flesh." It is the steward's responsibility to see that the flesh remains subjected to the **Spirit**. **Refer to John 4:24** as you explain this.

- Explain to the participants that the chain-of-command allows one to move up and down the hierarchical order without violating protocol. For further clarification, have the participants share the protocol or procedure on their jobs (or any organization they may belong) for accessing the company's or organization's head/president/CEO/owner directly.

- Read John 16:23, Mark 16:19, and Hebrews 4:16. Have the participants give feedback on how easy it is for them to access the Head in their business.

- Discuss with the participants the meaning of command, (1) "To direct with authority; give orders to; (2) To have control or authority over; rule." The American Heritage Dictionary of the English Language.

- In discussing the distribution of power within the business' chain-of-command, reiterate by reading as a whole group Matthew 6:33 and Proverbs 3:5-6, that the Head has **ultimate** power, control, and authority in the business. Following the Head in the chain-of-command is the Holy Spirit (Read John 14:15-18) and the spirit man (Read Luke 10:19). Angels are also a part of this chain (Read 1:14).

- Read Jeremiah 29:11, explain that the plan God has for Christians, His children, is one that truly secures success for their lives or **business**.

- The following are the answers to questions **1-11** in the workbook, and **#12** in the journal.

  1. life; Head, man, steward
  2. Father, Son, Holy Spirit
  3. connectedness
  4. love, merciful, gracious, forgiving, faithful; submission, obedience; strength, power
  5. steward
  6. spirit man
  7. Answers may vary, but the favorably response is; through spiritual means, as the Head and spirit man are spiritual beings, and through an on-going personal relationship with the Head.
  8. Answers may vary, but the favorably response is; the steward is the fleshly or physical part of the business and because of this, the Head cannot commune directly with the steward.
  9. Answers may vary, but the favorably responses are; (1) easy access to the Head which facilitates unobstructed communication, and (2) a clear delineated distribution

of power.

10. Answers may vary, but favorably responses are; the Head can be accessed easily by using the name of Jesus (John 16:23), who is seated at the right hand of the Father (Mark 16:19). The Head is also accessed through an open invitation (Hebrews 4:16).

11. The Head, Holy Spirit, the spirit man, and the angels.

12. In the diagram of the **Hierarchical Order**, a pictorial must indicate that the Head is first, followed by the spirit man, and lastly the steward. A brief description of each should also be included in the diagram. In the pictorial of the **Chain-of-Command**, once again it must indicate that the Head has ultimate authority, power and, control. The Holy Spirit and the spirit man follow the Head respectively, and the angels will be next. The diagram must indicate the flow of communication along the chain, and a brief description of how power and authority are distributed along the chain.

- End the session in prayer, thanking the Holy Spirit for His guidance.

*Lesson XI

Week XI

Standard Operating Procedures

Objective: To establish the order in which your business operates.

Tools Needed: Workbook, Bible, Pens, and Pencils

- Begin the session in prayer, ask the Holy Spirit to lead you and the group members into **all** truths.

- Explain to the participants that in establishing standard operating procedures for the business, they are essentially establishing ORDER by which the business will operate.

- As a group, read Galatians 5:17. After this reading, ask the participants if they were aware of these two forces existence? Discuss the two forces, and each forces' purpose, reiterate to the participants why it is important for ORDER to be established within their business/lives.

- As a group, read Psalms 51:5 and Galatians 5:19-21. Discuss the attributes of the sinful nature. Have some participants share their experience with the sinful nature.

- As a group read Galatians 5:22-23. Discuss the attributes and values of the Spiritual nature. **Stress** the importance of the power of the Spiritual nature to nullify the effects of being born in iniquity (Psalms 51:5).

- Review the three fundamental truths that the standard operating procedures must be built upon. **Truth #1**: Submit everything in your business to God. As a group read and discuss James 4:7. **Truth #2**: Let Jesus tame the beast (sinful nature) within. As a group read and discuss Paul's account in Romans 7:14-24. **Truth #3**: Realize the guaranteed victory given to you by God. As a group read and discuss I Corinthians 10:13.

- Review the journal exercise. Have the participants share some of the standard operating procedures they have created for the following principles; self-discipline, avoiding temptations, obedience and submission to the Head, and manifesting the fruits of the Spirit.

- Explain to the group participants that their primary **duties** and **responsibilities** within the business are centered on the three main service areas of worship, love, and witnessing. Refer to the workbook as you review each service area, read and discuss the related scripture/s.

- Review the related journal exercise. Have some participants share their responses.

- End the session in prayer, thanking the Holy Spirit for His guidance.

Lesson XII

Week XII

Quality Assurance

Objective: To understand the importance of ***accountability*** in a steward's life.

Tools Needed: Workbook, Bible, Pens, and Pencils

- Begin the session in prayer, ask the Holy Spirit to lead you and the group members into **all** truths.

- Read and discuss as a group Romans 14:12. Ask the question, "What is accountability, and why is it important? Stress the importance of being accountable for words spoken, and actions taken.

- Discuss the importance of having an accountability partner. Explain that this partner must be a Christian, Spirit-led, and Spirit-filled. One who manifests the fruits of the Spirit. The accountability partner is one who should in love, correct, redirect, and support. Have the participants think about one person whom he or she can have as an accountability partner. This person does not necessarily have to be in the group.

- Review and discuss the **Accountability Evaluation** with the group. Have participants give feedback.

- Review and discuss the **How Well Are You Tending Your Garden?** Exercise with the group. Participants should have completed this exercise. Have participants give feedback.

- Review and discuss the **Releasing It** exercise with the group. Have participants give feedback.

- End the session in prayer, thanking the Holy Spirit for His guidance.

H.O.P.E.

Holding Onto Positive Expectations

A Spiritual Journey Towards An Empowered Transformed Life

Workbook
(Journal Included)

Written by
Andrea J. Williams M.S.

Preface

This workbook is first and foremost an assignment from the Lord. In 2001, the Lord placed me in an environment where I served a population of people who for the most part presented as *hopeless*. As a result of this experience, I felt a strong compulsion to do something, because at a point and time in my life, I too was *very* hopeless. Fortunately, with the Lord's hand over my life, He led and guided me along a path where I was able to move beyond a life of hopelessness to a life of *complete* joy, hope, and fruitfulness. I wanted the same for the population I served. I was determined to work towards bridging the gap between the abyss of hopelessness, and the realization of attaining and living a fruitful and hopeful life.

Armed with this determination, various data gathering tools and intervention techniques, I was able to probe more into the root cause of this deep-seated feeling of hopelessness. I soon realized the problem stemmed from any one, or a combination of the following situations:

- Childhood trauma, or a traumatic event that was never resolved, and as a result the individual set out on his or her life's journey with a defeatist posture.
- An on-going losing battle with substance abuse and/or mental illness.
- A series of setbacks and disappointing events that seem to have crippled the individual's ability to think rationally, and act responsibly.
- A perpetuation of generational woes or curses.
- A decline in one's morals, values, and spirituality as a result of living a "lie" and/or a reprehensible lifestyle.

Using the information gathered, I, in conjunction with the guidance and grace of the Holy Spirit created this work of ***excellence***. I *strongly* believe the lessons and activities presented in this workbook will help those who are living life in a state of perpetual *hopelessness,* move away from their present state of being to a life that is ***spiritually transformed and empowered.***

I am not claiming to have the answers to all of life's problems, nor am I negating the valuable services of substance abuse and mental health counseling, Christian counseling preferably, if and when needed. However, I do believe "true" life-long change in one's life can ***only*** be achieved through the combination of **Divine Intervention**, and a sincere desire on one's behalf to wholeheartedly commit to, and embrace the process of change by faith and Spirit-led effort.

Introduction

If you are reading this workbook, you are probably in a state of hopelessness, a place of spiritual destitution. ***A place of nothingness***. It seems as if life has taken all it could have away from you. You are at that place in your life where nothing matters anymore; nothing hurts anymore, a place of sheer numbness.

As you think about your life thus far, do you find yourself asking one or more of the following questions?;

- *How did I allow myself to become addicted to drugs and or/ alcohol?*
- *Why did I allow myself to fall into the same traps or make the same mistakes of others, which I vowed I will never fall into or make?*
- *Why did those who were supposed to love, care for, and protect me sexually and/ or physically abuse me? Rendering me unable to trust others and enjoy healthy relationships.*
- *Why was I placed in foster care? Didn't my parent (s) love me enough to keep me?*
- *Who is my real father, and where is my mother?*
- *How did I end up at this place in my life? This was not supposed to happen to me.*
- *Why was I even born? I would have been better off dead.*

The purpose of this workbook is to challenge you to take what the enemy intended for evil, and allow Jesus to make *good* out of it. Allow Jesus to restore unto you the abundant life **He intended** for you to have. "The thief does not come except to steal, and to kill, and to destroy. I have come that they may have life, and that they may have it more abundantly." John 10:10 (NKJV, emphasis added) Allow Jesus to completely transform your life.

At this point, you are probably thinking "How can Jesus make good out of a life that has been totally destroyed by drugs and/or alcohol, a host of poor decisions, or years of destructive and reckless living?" "I even hate looking at myself in the mirror. I have lost *everything*, my children, my family, job/career, house, car, and **even** *myself*." "How can Jesus make good out of such a mess?"

You might even be at a place in your life where you are angry with God, because you feel He could have stopped all the *bad* things from happening to you. Many events in life can be most devastating and life altering. Such events are almost impossible to overcome, and as a result the memories of these events can be perpetually haunting. When this happens, it is very easy to fall into the pit of despair, discouragement, and self-pity. Eventually, you find that you have stopped believing that things could change for the better.

My friend, I have been down that road before. I experienced many painful events in my life, and I allowed the enemy the opportunity to use those events to take me on a course of destructive and reckless living for a period of time. I too, had gotten to the point where I was angry with God. I would spend countless hours in my miserable pity-party wondering why I had to go through what I was going through and what did I do to deserve such misery. I had stopped believing in God and in His desire and ability to change my life. ***Then,*** I came to my senses. I allowed Jesus to take all the mess in my life and make good out of it. Allow Jesus to do the same for you. He ***can*** and ***will*** transform your life. He did it for me; He will do it for you. Based on the principle of *sowing* and *harvesting*, this workbook focuses on your ability by faith, to realize a spiritually empowered, transformed life through maximizing your potential, and becoming the man or woman God predestined you to ***be***. See Jeremiah 29:11-12

Presented as a holistic approach to your victorious life in Jesus; this workbook is centered on the synergistic relationship that exists between your **M**ind, **B**ody, and your **S**pirit.

Your Mind: Satan knows that if you change your thinking, you will change your life; therefore, his primary *modus operandi* is to ***attack*** your mind. With his lies, he creates an infertile environment in your mind, which yields a life of mediocrity, barrenness, despair, and hopelessness. In part **I** of this workbook, you will explore the condition of your mind, and create with the help of the Holy Spirit a fertile environment in your mind; an environment that yields a life of ***complete*** fulfillment. It is in this environment you will be planting *your* positive seeds of expectation for your *entire* life.

Your Body: Many people struggle through life as a fragmented *mess.* They travel along life's journey feeling and *being* confused, frustrated, and disoriented. Are you one of those people? In part **II** of the workbook, you will become aware of *spiritual body intactness* through the concepts of **stewardship** and spiritual **wholeness**.

Your Spirit: Part **III** of this workbook takes you on a spiritual examination that will leave you spiritually grounded. You will identify your spiritual purpose, and its importance in you fulfilling your expectations and hope. You will also discover the essence of your being, your *spirit man*, and its significance in the spiritual part of your journey.

Finally, as you read through this workbook, completing all the exercises and activities in the workbook ***and*** the journal, I implore you to be truthful with yourself. In doing so, you will realize the positive expectations you have for your transformed life, and experience a bountiful harvest.

GARDEN OF H.O.P.E.

Holding Onto Positive Expectations

Garden of H.O.P.E.

Your Journey begins…

As you begin your process of transformation, I want you to reflect upon the beginning of creation. In the book of Genesis, you will find Adam beginning his life's journey in a garden. "Then the Lord God planted a garden in Eden…and there He placed the man He created." Genesis 2:8 (LASB)

Why did God place Adam in a garden? He could have placed Adam anywhere He wanted in Eden, but He chose to place Adam in a garden that the Lord himself planted in Eden. I believe this was God's way of demonstrating to us that a garden *was* and *still* is the ideal place for new beginnings. As you begin your scared journey towards your new beginning, you are going to find yourself in a garden, **your Garden Of H.O.P.E**. *This is where your journey begins.*

Throughout the course of your journey, there will be days of discouragement and despondency along the way. I know this as a fact. As the pressures of everyday life mounted there were many, many days I wanted to just give up on this particular seed I planted in my garden of H.O.P.E. But when I thought about the alternative, a life of mediocrity and barrenness, I persevered through the hardships and difficulties knowing that I was not alone. Through the grace and guidance of the Holy Spirit, I was able to realize my harvest. You are now experiencing that harvest, this workbook.

Whenever you feel like giving up, first know that you are not alone, and encourage yourself as I did, and as Jesus did the disciples with the following scripture. "…I assure you, even if you had faith as small as a mustard seed you could say to this mountain, "Move from here to there," and it would move. Nothing would be impossible." Matthew 17:20 (LASB)

This scripture encouraged me tremendously, to the point that I was prompted to seek out the actual size of a mustard seed. I wanted to see the amount of faith I needed to have to move the mountains of fear, confusion, despondency, frustration, discouragement, negativity, weariness, and insecurity out of my way. After seeing that a mustard seed was no bigger than the head of a dressmaker's pin, I knew I was able to press through anything!

What are the mountains that could impede your progress? Do not give any of them the opportunity to stop you from realizing your harvest. Memorize the above scripture, and whenever you experience hardships and difficulties, say the scripture out loud, and press on.

In your garden of H.O.P.E., your transformed life begins with you first gathering together all your positive seeds of expectation. Eventually, you are going to sow your seeds in a fertile environment, and watch them manifest into the harvest you *hoped* for.

Exercise: Think about what it means to you to have a spiritually empowered, *transformed* life. Imagine all the possibilities that await you. What are the expectations you hope to realize in your *new* life?

The expectations I have for my spiritually empowered, transformed life are

_____

_____

_____

_____

_____

_____

_____

_____

_____

_____

_____

Part One

Lessons 1 to 4

THE MIND

"…But we can understand these things, for we have the mind of Christ."
1 Corinthians 2:16

Satan's attacks come in many different ways. At times he will attack your physical body through sickness. Sometimes his attacks come through relationships, and at other times he may attack you through your finances. However, his most strategic and common method of attack is through the *mind.* Why? He knows that your transformed life (mind, body, and spirit) begins in your mind. "Don't copy the behavior and customs of this world, but let God transform you into a new person by changing the way you think..." Romans 12:2 (LASB) Satan knows that if he can get you off track in your mind, you will wreck your life just like a derailed train.

The dictionary and concordance of the Life Application Study Bible, defines the mind as, "that part of the human experience that engages in conscious thinking, feeling, and decision making." 1 This definition clearly identifies the mind as being a vital part of the human experience. In essence, you *are* or *can* become what you think. Therefore, it is most imperative that you become aware of, and understand the *make-up* of your mind. In doing so, you will begin to:

(1) *Uncover, confront, and conquer every thought that comes against you to create confusion, conflict, and chaos in your mind; and subsequently your life.*

(2) *Become empowered in your ability to overcome negative and inappropriate thinking; thereby, enabling you to make sound, godly, decisions.*

(3) *Most importantly, realize that there is a spiritual dimension to your mind, and it is in this spiritual dimension that you will be able to conquer the attacks of the enemy, satan.*

What is the make-up of your mind? I believe the best and simplest way to answer this question is to perceive your mind as a fertile or infertile medium. In a fertile medium, you will find productivity, as life thrives in such an environment. In an infertile medium, the exact opposite exists. There is no life, only barrenness.

Read Matthew 13:3-9 and 18-23. In the parable of the Four Soils, Jesus tells the story about a farmer who set out to sow grain or plant seeds. In this parable, seeds were planted in four different types of soil yielding different results. Using the same parable, you will become aware of the type of soil that constitutes your mind; thereby, revealing the "make-up" of your mind.

Read and summarize Matthew 13:3-9 and 18-23.

_____

_____

_____

_____

_____

_____

_____

_____

_____

Four Different Types of Soil

In the parable of the Four Soils, you find a farmer who had set out to plant some seeds. As he scattered his seeds, some fell on *hard* soil, some *rocky* soil, some *thorny* soil. All of these soils *rejected* the seeds that were sown into them. However, there was one soil type that the farmer sown his seed into that *accepted* the seeds planted in it. This was the *good* soil, and it was the **only** soil where the farmer was able to realize a bountiful harvest.

Type I; Hard Soil: In the parable, the hardened condition of the soil made it impossible for the seeds to penetrate into the ground, and as a result, the birds came along and ate the seeds. In His explanation of this parable, Jesus explained that the hardened soil represents those who hear about the Good News of the Kingdom of Heaven but lacks *understanding*, and eventually satan comes along and snatches the Good News away from their *hearts*. Note, in the Bible, *heart* is sometimes translated as *"mind"* or *"soul"*. 2

Is your mind made-up of hard soil? In the past, do you recall hearing about the Kingdom of Heaven and Its Good News? What did you do with this information? Did you allow it to fall by the wayside because you lacked ***understanding***? If you lack understanding, ask God for it, He **will** give it to you. "Understanding is a wellspring of life to him who has it..." Proverbs 16:22 (NKJV).

By accepting the Good News of ***salvation***, and becoming a citizen of the Kingdom of Heaven, you will be able to begin creating a fertile environment in your mind. Do not allow the enemy another opportunity to ruin your harvest by snatching your seeds away.

Type II; Rocky Soil: In this soil, the farmer planted his seeds; however, the young plants did not survive. The rocky condition of the soil did not allow their roots to penetrate deep into the ground, and the young plants were not able to receive the nourishment they needed to survive. Jesus explained that this parable represents those who hear and receive the message of the Good News with joy, but this joy is short-lived. As soon as problems or persecution come their way for believing, they wilt away, just like the young plants.

Is your mind made-up of rocky soil? This type of soil represents a lack of ***commitment***.

Once you have made a commitment to Christ, by receiving and accepting the message of the Good News, you have to be committed to persevere through *all* that may come your way. By persevering the hard times, you are allowing your roots to penetrate deeper and deeper into the Kingdom of Heaven; whereby, you will receive all the rights and protection promised to you by Christ, the sovereign Ruler of the Kingdom. This is the only way you are going to realize a fruitful and bountiful harvest in your life. Remember you *will* have problems. You are going to have trails and tribulations, but there is hope for you during those times, read John 16:33.

Type III; Thorny Soil. The seeds planted in this soil yielded young shoots that were choked out by the thorns. Jesus explained that this type of soil represents those who hear and accept the Good News, but soon become distracted by the cares and wealth of life.

Is your mind made-up of thorny soil? Are you easily *distracted*? Once you have accepted the Good News from Christ, and have made the commitment to follow and trust Him as He leads and guides you through the process of a renewed, transformed life, *do not* allow the cares or wealth of this world to distract you. Once you do, thorns *will* choke out your seeds of expectation.

Type IV; Good Soil: The seeds that were planted in good, *fertile* soil produced a bountiful harvest. This is the only soil of all soil types where the farmer was able to realize a harvest that produced up to one hundred times what he planted. Jesus explained that this soil represents those who *truly* accept the Good News of Christ.

Is your mind made-up of good soil? Can you *truly* say you possess a mind that is fertile and productive at this point in time? If you cannot admit to having a productive, fertile mind at this time, after completing lessons one through four, you *will* be able to do so. And you will be able to produce a bountiful harvest.

Lesson I

What Type of Soil Is Your Mind?

A Closer Examination

What is the make-up of your mind? Do you possess a fertile or infertile medium? A closer look at the four soil types in the parable revealed three infertile mediums and one fertile one. The hard soil represents a mind that lacks *understanding*; the rocky soil is one that lacks *commitment*; and the thorny soil lacks focus and is easily *distracted*. All three of these infertile mediums produced ***nothing***. However, the good soil, the *only* fertile medium, was **truly** accepting of Christ's Good News, and it was ***only*** this medium that was able to produce a one hundredfold harvest.

Complete the following exercise:

1. At this point in time in my life's journey, the make-up of my mind soil is the _____ _____ soil type a/an _____ medium.
2. For the past five years of my life, I have operated with this type of mind soil, and have yielded the following results in the various areas listed:

Personal: _____
_____
_____
_____

Family: _____
_____
_____
_____

Work: _____
_____
_____
_____

Finances: _____

_____   _____
_____
_____

Spiritual: _____

_____
_____
_____

Recreation/Leisure: _____

_____
_____

Look over the exercise you have just completed. If you have been operating and functioning with an infertile medium, you have already experienced first hand the kind of harvest such a medium will yield. Are you now ready to begin the process of creating a fertile medium, *good* mind soil in which you will eventually be planting your seeds of expectation? Then, move on to the next lessons.

Lesson II

Tilling the Soil: Plowing and Harrowing

Any experienced farmer will tell you that in order for there to be a bountiful harvest, the soil he/she plants in *must* be prepared for raising crops. This preparation phase is called tilling. Tilling soil requires three important steps; plowing, harrowing, and fertilizing. Plowing, the first step breaks up the soil and prepares it for sowing by cutting furrows in the soil. Harrowing further breaks up the soil, and then evens off the plowed soil. Fertilization is the mixing of fertilizer into the soil, thereby adding nutrients into the soil.

Step I

Plowing

As you begin the tilling process through the plowing phase, be prepared! This part of the tilling process is most impacting. It is the initial breaking up of your mind soil. In the plowing phase, you will begin the process of becoming *loosened* and *disconnected* from many familiar things, places, and people in your life. Your comfort zone is going to receive a substantial amount of shaking and breaking up. This *loosening* and *disconnecting* is most vital if you plan on creating a fertile medium in which to plant your seeds of expectation, and if you plan on experiencing a fruitful and bountiful harvest.

From the list below, place a **(x)** next to all that *need* to be loosened and disconnected from your mind soil.

Non-Productive Thoughts ( ): Do you find yourself thinking about things that are of **no** value or help to you, and your well being? Loosen and disconnect yourself from these thoughts, or spend countless hours torturing yourself.

Negative Thinking ( ): What type of negative thoughts have invaded and taken captive of your mind? Do you find yourself always focusing on the worst that could happen in situations, circumstances, and people, instead of focusing on the positive possibilities? Read Philippians 4:8 to see what the Word tells you to think about.

Friends and Associates ( ): "Can two walk together, unless they are agreed?" Amos 3:3 (NKJV) Every friendly face you meet is **NOT** a friend. Your friends should be traveling along the same pathway that you are. True friends do not lead you to your damnation and destruction. Remember, association inevitably bears assimilation.

Unhealthy Relationships ( ): Unhealthy relationships are those that are toxic to your *well being.* Do you find yourself always being the doormat in your relationships? Do you find that you are always compromising your values, morals, needs, spirituality, and self-worth for the sake of maintaining a relationship? If you answered "yes" to any of these questions, then, you have experienced or are experiencing an unhealthy relationship or relationships.

Destructive Behaviors ( ): Read Galatians 5:19-21 your behavior *does* matter! It is the differences between you living a victorious or a defeated life. Loosen and disconnect yourself from all the destructive behaviors that you have engaged, and are engaged in. Such behaviors, if you continue to practice them will destroy you and your harvest.

Family Members ( ): "and a man's enemies will be those of his own household." Matthew 10:36 (NKJV) Some family members are going to be supportive of you and your efforts toward experiencing a transformed and renewed life in Christ Jesus, on the other hand, some are going to reject you completely. Do not be dismayed; the word of God warned you that this would happen. Just shake loose and disconnect from those family members and put them in God's hand.

Tradition ( ): Traditions have shaped lives for centuries. Unfortunately, not all traditions passed down from generation to generation are functional. Many people have adhered to, and have lived their lives by these *dead* traditions, and as a result, their lives have become stymied, unsatisfied, and unfruitful. What traditions have you allowed to stymie your growth? Loosen and disconnect from them all.

Step II

Harrowing

The next step is to harrow the soil of your mind. In this part of the tilling process, more breaking up of the soil is required, after that, the soil is then "*evened*" off. This phase of the process demands **patience**, **time**, and **diligence**. It has to be done thoroughly because you are preparing a fertile **environment** in which to plant your seeds of expectation.

Journal Exercise: For each item you placed a **(X)** next to in the plowing exercise, briefly describe each one by going through the harrowing process. You will further *"break up"* your mind soil through *internalizing*, and *"even off"* through seeking *resolution*. As you complete this exercise, follow my personal harrowing experience below. For years I harbored non-productive thoughts, through *internalization*, I accepted the fact that life **is** not fair. I evened off my mind soil through the *resolution* that the pain and suffering I received, made me a stronger person.

Example: Non-Productive Thoughts

Most of my thoughts during my late childhood and early adult life were non-productive as a result of the hurts, pain, shame, and humiliation inflicted upon me by some family members, friends, and associates. Through the plowing phase, I loosened and disconnected myself from these thoughts. By accepting the fact that life can be unfair at times (Matthew 5:45), I was able to "***even off***" my mind soil. I was no longer tortured by feelings of revenge, grudges, bitterness, or hatred. In the harrowing phase, I also came to the realization that even though life was unfair to me, it was still very favorable to me. It was those experiences that molded me into the strong Christian woman I am today. Thank God!

Lesson III

Tilling the Soil: Fertilization

Do you believe you are ready to move onto the fertilization phase? If not, take all the time you need to fully complete the plowing and harrowing phase of the tilling process. To move onto this final stage of the tilling process without completing the work of plowing and harrowing, *will* be counterproductive to you manifesting the harvest of your expectation. However, if you believe you are ready to move onto the fertilization phase, then, it is time for you to begin to *fertilize* your mind soil, and *prepare* it to plant your seeds of expectation.

In this part of the tilling process, you will be providing the initial life source for your seeds of expectation to thrive in. This life source, your fertilizer is your *complete acceptance* of the *Good News* about the Kingdom, and your total belief and trust in God to transform your life.

In preparation for the planting of your seeds, complete the imagery exercise below. Take your time with this exercise. To enhance this experience, complete this excercise when you are in a restful and peaceful state, and are able to retreat to a place of solitude for forty-five minutes to one hour.

Imagery Exercise: Take a deep dreath; hold it for a second and release. Repeat. Prayerfully, ask the Lord to fill you with his peace and grace as you complete this excercise.

> Visualize your Garden of H.O.P.E. plowed and harrowed. As you walk throughout your garden barefooted, feel the soil beneath your feet and between your toes. Walk down each row slowly spreading the fertilizer as you go, appreciate the fertile environment you have created in your mind with the help of the Holy Spirit. When you have reached the end of the last row; **STOP**. Stoop down and pick up a handful of soil, look at how loose, contaminant-free, and enriched it appears. Now allow the soil to fall back to the ground through your fingers. Visualize the harvest you are expecting, see how lush, green, and bountiful it appears. Now say to yourself, "By faith, I believe and receive this harvest, in Jesus' Name, Amen."

Now, close your eyes and recapture the imagery of your lush, green and bountiful garden for five minutes.

Review the expectations you have for your spiritually, empowered, transformed life, this is the very first exercise you completed in this workbook. These expectations *are* your positive seeds of expectation, and these are the seeds you will be planting in your **now** fertile mind, which *is* your **Garden of H.O.P.E.**

Exercise: On the lines below list those positive seeds of expectation you will be planting in your Garden of H.O.P.E.

Seeds of Expectation

_____   _____
_____   _____
_____   _____
_____   _____
_____   _____
_____   _____
_____   _____
_____   _____

You are *now* ready to plant your seeds of expectation. In your journal turn to the "Planting Your Seeds of Expectation" exercise, and **Plant your seeds!**

And whatever things you ask in prayer, believing, you will receive."
Matthew 21:22 (NKJV)

Lesson IV

Tending the Garden

Caution! Unless you are convinced your mind soil is fertile ground to plant your seeds of expectation in, you are not ready to move onto this lesson. If you need more time in the tilling process, take all the time you need, ***you will not regret it.***

The tilling is completed, great job! In order to secure the integrity of the fertile environment you have created in your mind, you will have to care for your garden with great diligence. Over the next eight weeks you will tend to your garden by *watering, weeding, fertilizing*, and *safeguarding* it. Each activity is significant in and of itself, as well as collectively.

Watering Your Garden: Watering your garden regularly is essential for the life of your seeds. However, too much water or too little water is not good. Do you find yourself overly anxious about the journey you have embarked upon? If you are, you are in danger of watering your garden too much. On the other hand, if you are feeling fearful and doubtful about the journey, you may be in danger of not watering your seeds enough. An overall feeling of peace indicates you are applying the right amount of water to your seeds of expectation. "Be anxious for nothing, ...and the peace of God, which surpasses all understanding, will guard your hearts and minds through Christ Jesus." Philippians 4:6-7 (NKJV)

Weeding Your Garden: Weeding your garden is vital! If you do not, your garden *will* be over taken by pesky invaders such as anxiety, fear, doubt, insecurity, self-pity, impatience, laziness, procrastination, a lack of confidence, poor self-worth, low self-esteem, guilt, worry, and shame. These invaders, along with a host of many others will choke the life out of your garden of H.O.P.E. Beware! Do not allow your garden to become invaded by weeds, as soon as you notice them pull them out from the root up.

Fertilizing the Garden: As you continue to hold onto the Good News of the Kingdom, trusting and believing in Christ, you *will* maintain the life of your garden. "Without wavering, let us hold tightly to the hope we say we have, for God can be trusted to keep his promises." Hebrews 10:23 (LASB) Regular maintenance in this area is evidenced by spiritual maturity; a lack of maintenance in this area is evidenced by the exact opposite, spiritual stagnation.

Safeguarding Your Garden: Safeguarding your garden against intruders will definitely extend the life of your expectations. It will also help you maintain your fertile environment. The most dangerous intruder you must safeguard your garden against is other people's opinion. Others are entitled to their opinions; however, this journey you have embarked upon to accept the Good News of Christ, and allow Him to transform your life completely is a personal experience. Do not allow the negative and careless opinions of others the opportunity to thwart your efforts, and shatter all your H.O.P.E.s. The moment you do, you will have to till your garden all over again, and re-plant your seeds of expectations.

Exercise: In your journal complete the exercise, **"How Well Are You Tending Your Garden?"**

Part Two

Lessons 5 to 8

THE BODY

"You made all the delicate, inner parts of my body and knit me together in my mother's womb. Thank you for making me so wonderfully complex! Your workmanship is marvelous…"
Psalm 139:13-14

The four lessons in this section focus on spiritual body intactness through the concepts of *stewardship* and *spiritual wholeness*. From the perspective of a steward; you will explore spiritual wholeness in the areas of relationship, personal growth, life success, and health.

Stewardship

"Or don't you know that your body is the temple of the Holy Spirit, who lives in you and was given to you by God? You do not belong to yourself, for God bought you with a high price. So you must honor God with your body." I Corinthians 6:19-20

This scripture clearly states that your body belongs to God. It is not yours to do as you please; you are only the steward of it. The American Heritage Dictionary defines a steward as, "one who manages another's property, finances, or affairs." This definition, in conjunction with the above scripture lead to one conclusion, you are simply managing **God's property**, your body.

Until I became aware of this revelation that my body belonged to God, I was under the impression that I was the boss and owner of my body. Because of this misassumption, I misused and violated the members of my body for many years. My life was a total wreck! As I grew in my spiritual walk with the Lord, I gained the knowledge about stewardship. I learned that as a steward, my time, finances, gifts, talents, praise, worship, and ultimately my life *all* belong to God. I realized that I had to relinquish my claim of ownership and become the steward that I needed to be. As a result of this, I began to function in God's body with great proficiency, and was able to achieve a level of *wholeness* I never experienced before.

Exercise: Read I Corinthians 6:19-20, and the definition of a steward again. Write your reaction to the revelation that your body does not belong to you.

_____

_____

_____

Spiritual Wholeness

Society's idea of wholeness is completely different from the spiritual view on wholeness. In society one is considered *whole* when one has maximized one's potential in the areas of one's education, finances, vocation, possessions, and overall well being. Moreover, the ability to attain such wholeness from societal perspective is often accredited to the individual's *sole* efforts.

On the other hand, the spiritual view on wholeness centers on an intertwined relationship that exists between the Creator and the created, God and mankind. Spiritual wholeness says, "Yes, I am the vine; you are the branches. Those who remain in me, and I in them, will produce **much** fruit. For apart from me you can do nothing...But if you stay joined to me and my words remain in you, you may ask any request you like, and it will be granted! My true disciples produce **much** fruit. This brings great glory to my Father." John 15:5, 7-8 (LASB, emphasis added) Wholeness then becomes a matter of being *complete* in Christ Jesus, and not in mankind's own efforts or abilities.

How is this completeness attained? It is achieved through mankind's *total* dependence upon, and co-existence with the Lord. A good and faithful steward realizes that being *complete* can only be achieved through the relationship that exists between the Creator and the created. The Creator knows what He created; therefore, He is able to lead, guide, protect, and direct what He created with impeccable precision and handling. The created on the other hand is incapable of achieving completeness or *true* wholeness. He or she does not have all the information needed to do so, and to place trust in the flesh's ability to become **all** that God wants His created beings to be, and to possess **all** that God has in store for the created would be folly. See Philippians 3:3.

Exercise: How do the two perspectives on *wholeness* differ from each other?

_____

_____

_____

_____

_____

_____

_____

_____

_____

_____

_____

Lesson V
Relationships

The most important relationship in your life that you *must* establish or re-establish is the one that exists between you and your Creator. Read John 15:5-8 again, Jesus refers to those who produce much fruit as his true disciples. To be able to produce a *fruitful harvest* in your life, **you have to be a disciple of Jesus;** you must have a relationship with Him. Do you have a relationship with Him?

To have a relationship with the Lord, you have to be a born-again believer. Are you a born-again believer? Being born-again simply means you believe that Jesus is the Son of God, and that He died for your sins; and with a contrite and broken spirit, you have asked the Lord Jesus to come into your life, and be your Lord and Savior. If you are not a born-again believer, and are desirous of a relationship with the Lord, God Almighty, take this time now to pray this prayer:

Father God, I come before you a sinner. I repent of my sins; forgive me Lord. I believe that Jesus is the Son of God, and that He died for my sins. Come into my life, and be my Lord and Savior. Teach me how to love and serve you with all my heart, mind, and soul. I thank you. In Jesus' name I pray. Amen.

If you said that prayer and believed it, you *are* a born-again believer. You may recall praying a similar prayer in the past, but are presently living in a back-slidden condition. If this is your case, you can re-establish your relationship with the Lord by simply acknowledging that you are in such a condition. Ask the Lord for forgiveness, receive it, and serve the Lord with a whole heart from the moment you reaffirm the commitment you made to the Lord when you first became a born-again believer.

The second important relationship that you must establish or re-establish in your life is that with your **"self."** That part of you that exists within the depths of your being; that part of you that is separated from the outside world, where you still experience fleeting bouts of childlike innocence and vulnerability; that part of you that yearns to truly **BE.**

Like many others, you have probably neglected to cultivate and/or maintained this relationship. It is very easy to get caught up in the busyness of life, being what others want you to be, and doing for everyone else, without taking the time to assess where your "self" fits into the affairs of your life. Before long, you find your "self" asking these questions; "Who am I *really?*" and "*How* and *where* did I lose my "self?" Take a few minutes to think about these questions and complete the exercise below.

Exercise: Describe the type of relationship that exists between you and your "self." Would you say that it is (1) Nonexistent, (2) Casual, or (3) Intimate? Explain your answer.

_____

_____

_____

_____

_____

_____

_____

_____

_____

Establishing or Re-Establishing a Relationship With Your "Self"

How do you go about the task of establishing or re-establishing a relationship with your "self?" The *first* step is to look at your "self" in relation to all the relationship types and roles that it occupies and functions in. The *second* step is to examine the expectations and demands placed upon each role. Is the "self" capable of meeting the expectations and demands placed upon it? The *third* step in establishing or re-establishing a relationship with your "self" is to redefine the "self;" in doing so, you will reveal your "true self." The "self" you were created to **be.** This reconnecting and/or *finding* of the "true self" is very important. You need to know who you really are from deep within the core of your being. Your "self" needs to be firmly anchored. As a responsible steward, it is incumbent upon you to have *your* affairs in order, before you are able to administer to the affairs of others. **Remember, you cannot give others what your "self" does not have!**

Step I

You may not have thought about all the relationship types your "self" occupies and functions in before now. The "self" has been *multitasking* for years! With each relationship type, there is/are corresponding role or roles that the "self" is obligated to assume, whether it wants to or not. You will explore these role or roles further in step II. By completing the exercise below, you will have a visual of all the relationship types and corresponding role or roles that your "self" occupies and functions in.

Exercise: Check all the relationship types, and **circle** each corresponding role/s your "self" occupies and functions in.

Andrea J. Williams M.S.

Relationship Types	**Roles**
( ) Parental	mother, father, grandparent, step/foster mother, step/foster father step/foster grandparent
( ) Sibling	brother, sister, step/foster brother step/foster sister
( ) Platonic	friend, associate
( ) Intimate	husband, wife, fiancé, girlfriend, boyfriend
( ) Familial	aunt, uncle, cousin, in-laws
( ) Child	son, daughter, grandchild, foster/step child
( ) Professional	employer, employee, supervisor, administrator, co-worker

Step II

In this step, you will examine the various roles the "self" assumes, and the expectations and demands placed upon it. Is the "self" capable of satisfying the demands and expectations of each role it assumes? Occupying and functioning in a relationship type is not enough. For example, you can occupy or function in the *parental* relationship type, **but** still not satisfy the expectations and demands of the role of mother or father. Any man or woman could become a parent, but it takes a father/mother to *raise* a child.

In establishing or re-establishing a relationship with your "self" it is extremely important to know the demands and expectations placed upon the "self," and whether or not the "self" is capable of meeting these demands and expectations. This evaluation will assist in increasing "self" **awareness**, a quality that is essential in the "true self."

Exercise: From the exercise above, list *all* the roles you assume. Describe the expectations and demands attached to each role that *your* "self" is required to meet.

Role: _____

Expectations and Demands: _____
_____
_____
_____
_____

Role: _____

Expectations and Demands: _____
_____
_____
_____
_____

Role: _____

Expectations and Demands: _____
_____
_____
_____
_____

Role: _____

Expectations and Demands: _____
_____
_____
_____
_____

Role: _____

Expectations and Demands: _____
_____
_____
_____
_____

Role: _____

Expectations and Demands: _____
_____
_____

_____

_____

Role: _____

Expectations and Demands: _____

_____

_____

_____

_____

Role: _____

Expectations and Demands: _____

_____

_____

_____

_____

Role: _____

Expectations and Demands: _____

_____

_____

_____

_____

*Role: _____

Expectations and Demands: _____

_____

_____

_____

_____

*If you need more space for this exercise, you will find it in your journal.

Upon completion of this exercise, review *carefully*. For each role that you assume, identify by circling *__only__* those demands and expectations that you are **truly** capable of meeting.

Step III
Re-Defining Your "Self": Discovering Your "True" SELF

The third step in establishing or re-establishing a relationship with your "self" is to *re-define* your "self;" and in doing so, you *will* discover your *true* "self."

For many years I failed miserably in my attempts to administer to the needs of my husband, children, family members, friends, and as strange as it may seem, my "self." In desperation, I began the quest of seeking the answers as to *why?* Why was I unable to meet the needs of others, and even my "self"? In this search, I was lead by the Holy Spirit to the revelation of the **"Self Wheel."**

Through the wheel, He showed me that I was living a lie. I was attempting to meet needs and expectations that I could not remotely satisfy. I had a false sense of identity, and did not know who my "true" self was. I confronted this issue and was able to (1) become aware of, and identify the *false* "self" image I operated and functioned in, and (2) eradicate the "false" self image forever, by activating the true "self", all by the grace of God. This experience gave me *great* freedom and liberty. Liberty to be the person God designed and predestined me to be, thereby, allowing me to truly administer to the needs of others, and those of my "self."

The Self-Wheel

The self-wheel, in essence, is how the "self" operates. The "self," which is comprised of the "false" and "true" self is at the center of the wheel, the hub. The wheel's spokes are the various relationship types and roles of the "self," and it is rimmed with expectations and demands. Dynamic energy between the "self," its relationship types, and roles generates at the hub. (See Fig. A)

Self-Wheel
Fig. A

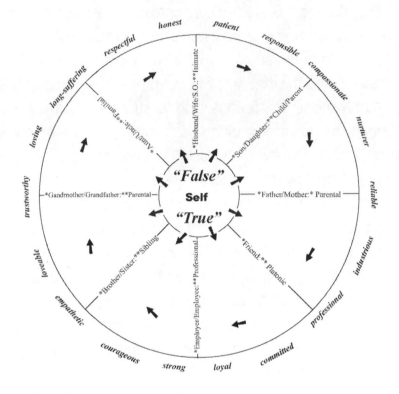

*Indicates (Roles)
**Indicates (Retionship Type)

The "False" Self

From childhood, demands and expectations were placed upon you by your parents, teachers, other persons of authority or influence, the environment, *and* society in regards to the ways in which you were to ***think***, ***speak***, and ***act.*** Consequently, your awareness of "self" was primarily shaped and defined by others, tradition, society, and the environment in which you lived; hence, the emergence of the "false" self. The "false" self emerged at childhood, operated and functioned as the predominant "self" throughout your childhood, and for the most part, continued to do so throughout your adult life. This is the reason why the "self" finds itself in a crisis many times. Until the "self" is re-defined in *Spirit* and in *Truth*, there will always be persistent and continuous manifestations of confusion, chaos, and deception throughout one's life.

The "True" Self

The "true" self is ever present. It simply lies dormant for as long as the "false" self is operating and functioning in a person's life. The "true" self is grounded in **The Truth** (The Word of God), it is wise and understanding. It is also most acquainted with its inventory. Therefore, it knows what it *can* and *cannot* give to, or do for others. It knows and acknowledges its strengths and limitations. However, when necessary it seeks its resources from the Lord because of the reassurance given in Philippians 4:13. The "true" self is grounded in its spiritual beliefs, values, and convictions. It expends energy, and manages its resources spiritually and judiciously. But most importantly, the "true" self recognizes and understands, that its most important relationship type is that of **Child of the Living God**, and its most important role is that of **steward**.

Activation of the "true" self will *completely* eradicate the presence and life of the "false" self. Its activation is also an integral part of the process towards a spiritually empowered life. (See Fig. B)

Self-Wheel
Fig. B

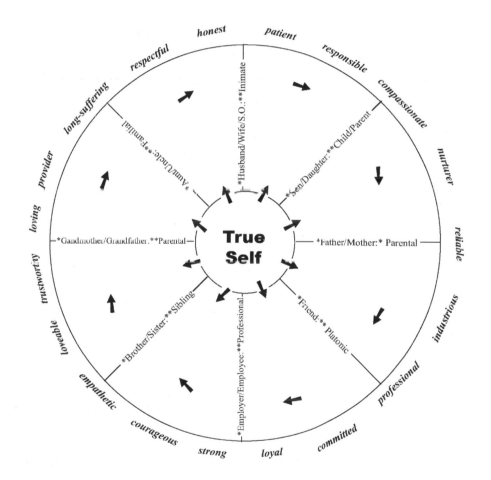

*Indicates (Roles)
**Indicates (Retionship Type)

Relationship Types and Roles

As mentioned earlier, the spokes of the wheel are the various relationship types and roles of the "self." With each relationship type, there are corresponding roles the "self" has to assume. For example, the parental relationship type requires you to assume the role of father, mother, or grandparent. Upon assuming a role, the "self" then attempts to satisfy or satisfies the duties and responsibilities assigned to that particular role. (See Fig. A)

Expectations and Demands

The wheel is rimmed with expectations and demands that the "self" is required to meet. If you assume the role of mother, in performing the duties and responsibilities of a mother, some of the expectations are to provide food, clothing, and shelter for your child or children, and a demand may be to successfully maintain a career and *home* at the same time.

Dynamic Energy

Dynamic energy between the "self," its relationship types, and roles is generated at the hub of the wheel. This energy is in **constant** motion, as the "self" operates and functions in various relationship types, assumes different roles, and attempts to satisfy many expectations and demands placed upon it simultaneously. For example, the mother in the parental relationship type, who has a job outside the home will move into the professional relationship type, and assume the role of employer or employee, satisfying the expectations and demands of that particular role.

Burn-Out and Inertia

Burn-out occurs when the "self" becomes incapacitated. The "false" self has ran its course, and the "true" self still remains dormant. The "false" self finally realizes it cannot operate and function as it once did. Skill has taken it as far as it could, for it *never* had what it needed to sustain itself.

Inertia is an extension of burn-out. It occurs when you continue in your attempts to operate and function in the vain efforts of the "false" self. However, you eventually end up spinning your wheel expending useless energy. Inertia can go on for years.

Recovery: Activation of the "True" Self

When you have been living a lie for so long, there comes a time in your life when you experience a crucial, frightening, but yet profound moment. This was where I experienced my *crossroad* moment. It was at this particular moment that I realized what I had perceived to be real in my life was actually *false*, and what I was predestined to become, the truth about who I really was appeared. In that moment I had to make a decision, whether I was going to continue to live a lie, or whether I was going to walk into the "true" me. I chose the latter, and began to move in the direction of my "true" self. Movement of my self-wheel began again, *and* this time it was useful energy expenditure. The "true" self was activated, and the "false" self was destroyed *forever.*

Discovering Your "True" Self

The following exercises will help you become acquainted with your "true" self.

A. <u>Identifying Your Strengths and Limitations</u>

By identifying your strengths and weaknesses, you will be laying down the foundation for a victorious life in Christ Jesus. The enemy often uses your areas of limitations to set you up for failure. By identifying these areas, you will be able to withstand the attacks of the enemy when he tries to tempt you in your limitations. Another benefit of becoming aware of your strengths and limitations is, you become most knowledgeable about what you *can* and *cannot* extend towards others as you transition in and out of different relationship types and roles.

List all your Strengths and Limitations

Strengths	Limitations
_____	_____
_____	_____
_____	_____
_____	_____
_____	_____
_____	_____
_____	_____
_____	_____
_____	_____

B. <u>Identifying Your Beliefs and Values</u>

Your family of origin, culture, environment, teachers, friends, religion, and various experiential events you have had throughout the course of your life, have all influenced and helped construct your belief and value systems. By taking a *closer* look at your values, beliefs, and the source or influential agent that is responsible for constructing your beliefs and values, you will be able to re-evaluate them, and *align* them with the beliefs and values of your **"true"** self.

Exercise: In the following exercise, place a check next to each item you **do** or **do not** value. Describe your **belief** about each item, and identify the **source**. I have completed an example for you to follow.

Example: Family (√) (Value) I value family a lot. **(Belief)** Even though my mother was a *very* strict disciplinarian, the one word we *always* heard in our household was "love," and because of this, I grew up believing in family, especially my family. Besides salvation, I believe the **family** is the second greatest gift from God to us. **(Source)** The source of this great value for, and belief in family came from my mother.

1. Family ( ) Value ( ) Do Not Value

Belief: _____

_____

_____

_____

Source: _____

_____

_____

_____

2. Relationship ( ) Value ( ) Do Not Value

Belief: _____

_____

_____

_____

Source: _____

_____

_____

_____

3. Religion ( ) Value ( ) Do Not Value

Belief: _____

_____

_____

_____

Source: _____

_____

_____

4. Friendship ( ) Value ( ) Do Not Value

Belief: _____

_____

_____

_____

Source: _____

_____

_____

_____

5. Children ( ) Value ( ) Do Not Value

Belief: _____

_____

_____

_____

Source: _____

_____

_____

_____

6. Education ( ) Value ( ) Do Not Value

Belief: _____

_____

_____

_____

Source: _____

_____

_____

_____

7. Work ( ) Value ( ) Do Not Value

Belief: _____

_____

_____

_____

Source: _____

_____

_____

_____

8. Money ( ) Value ( ) Do Not Value

Belief: _____

_____

_____

_____

Source: _____

_____

_____

_____

9. Sex ( ) Value ( ) Do Not Value

Belief: _____

_____

_____

_____

Source: _____

_____

_____

_____

10.   Health ( ) Value ( ) Do Not Value

Belief: _____

_____

_____

_____

Source: _____

_____

_____

_____

11.   Leisure ( ) Value ( ) Do Not Value

Belief: _____

_____

_____

_____

Source: _____

_____

_____

_____

Review the exercise you just completed, what are your values? How many of your beliefs are spiritually grounded? The more spiritually grounded they are, the more they are going to align with **The Truth**, a quality of your **"true"** self. In the example I gave, I indicated that I do value "family," and I was able to see that my belief in "family" was spiritually grounded because it did align with the *truth* of my "True Self." The *truth* in my "True Self" knew that it was my mother's duty and responsibility to discipline and guide me and my siblings in the right direction. The Word (**The Truth**) of God says, "Train up a child in the way he should go, And when he is old he will not depart from it." Proverbs 22:6 (NKJV) Even though the punishments were harsh at times, I knew my mother did it out of *love* and concern for me and my siblings, her family.

As you re-evaluate your belief and value systems, and begin to align your beliefs with the *truth* of your "true" self, take a look at what the **Word** says. Below you will find some scriptures for each area of value; these scriptures are to be used as a guide to help you become more spiritually grounded in your beliefs. You may find others scriptures that will support your beliefs as I did in my example of the family. The key point is that your beliefs and values are spiritually grounded.

Value: Family
Scripture: Colossians 3: 18-21
Value: Relationships
Scripture: Genesis 2:18
Value: Religion
Scripture: James 1:26-27

Value: Friendship
Scripture: Ecclesiastes 4:9-12 and Proverbs 18:24
Value: Children
Scripture: Psalm 127:3
Value: Education
Scripture: Proverbs 1:7 Once you receive *this* knowledge, your mind will be prepared to receive all types of knowledge. You will excel and be prosperous in all you do, because you will fear God and do HIS will.
Value: Work
Scripture: 2 Thessalonians 3:10
Value: Money
Scripture: I Timothy 6:10 NOTE: Money itself is not evil; it is the love of money that causes problems.
Value: Sex
Scripture: I Corinthians 6:18-20 and 1 Thessalonians 4:3-4; 7-8
Value: Health
Scripture: Proverbs 3:7-8, Proverbs 12:18, and I Corinthians 6:19-20
Value: Leisure
Scripture: 1 John 2:15-17

C. Defining Your "true" Self

You have identified all the relationship types you occupy, the roles you assume, and the demands and expectations that you are truly capable of satisfying. You have also identified your strengths and limitations, values, and beliefs. You are now ready to define your "true" self.

Exercise: Part I. Using the Self Wheel, (see Fig. C) define your "true" self. On the wheel, indicate the relationship types you occupy, the roles you assume, and the demands and expectations that you are truly capable of satisfying.

Fig. C Part II. Journal Exercise. In your journal complete the "True" Self essay.

My "True" Self Wheel

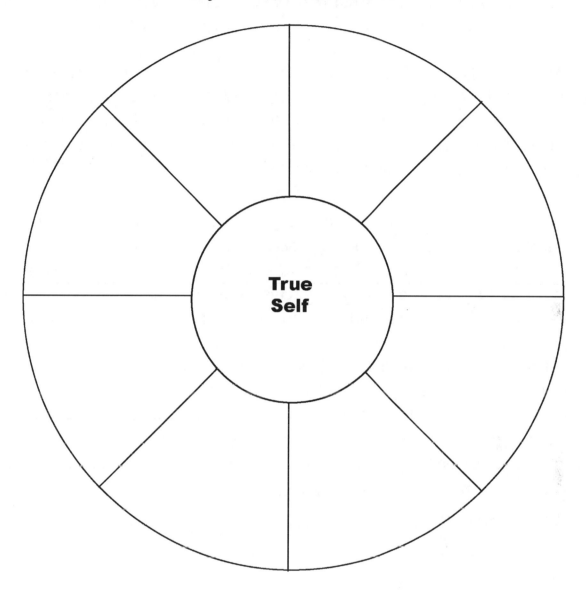

Lesson VI
Personal Growth

"...but to those who use well what they are given, even more will be given. But from those who are unfaithful, even what little they have will be taken away. "

Luke 19:26 (LASB)

As a steward of the life that was granted to you by God, you are responsible for personal growth in your life. You have been blessed with gifts and talents to necessitate such growth. You are ***not*** to remain stagnant. When you honor and glorify God with your gifts and talents you will find that you have placed yourself in the position to experience personal growth because you will be maximizing your life's potential.

What Are Your Gifts and Talents?

Webster's New World Dictionary defines *gift* as, "a natural ability;" and *talent* as, "any natural ability and power, or a superior ability in an art, etc." Each definition refers to a *natural* ability. The definition of talent even goes on to refer to a *superior* ability in one area or another. What an awesome God we serve! Even before you were born the Lord blessed you with natural abilities and/or superior abilities in various areas to help you function and succeed in this world.

What are your gifts and talents? To answer this question, take a few minutes to think about the area or areas that you are a *natural,* or have a *superior ability* in. You may have heard others say that they were born to sing, teach, preach, write, help others, etc. If you had to say you were born to *do* something, what would that be? By answering this question, you would begin to tap into your gifts and talents.

Complete the following sentences:

1. I was born to _____

_____

_____

_____

2. I am a natural when it comes to _____

_____

_____

_____

3. I have a superior ability in _____

_____

_____

_____

4. The areas I am gifted and talented in are _____

_____

_____

_____

5. I can honor and glorify God with my gifts and talents by

_____

_____

_____

Journal Exercise: In your journal write a complete plan of action for the development and actualization of your gifts and talents. Be specific. Be encouraged.

Character Building

Another important component of personal growth is *character building*. Maximizing your potential in the area or areas of your gifts and talents will reap a great harvest in your life; however, having a sound character will afford you the opportunity to reap an even greater and substantial harvest.

A man or woman of sound character is one who epitomizes **integrity, Read Proverbs 11:3**. A man or woman of sound character also bears the spirits of love, joy, patience, peace, kindness, goodness, faithfulness, gentleness, and **self-control. Read Galatians 5:22-23**.

Where are you in terms of your character? Do not be discouraged if you find that you possess a few or none of the spiritual attributes mentioned above. Note the word "building" in character building; you are a work in progress. The exercise below is designed to help you become a man or woman of sound character. I will be the first to admit that some, if not all of the tasks may present as challenging at first, but with persistence and perseverance, you will get through it.

Exercise: Over the next five weeks, you will focus on two spiritual attributes per week. Each attribute has a task for you to accomplish throughout the week, and accompanying scripture or scriptures for you to read and meditate upon. In your journal record your experiences daily.

Week 1
Attributes: Integrity and Love

Attribute: Integrity

Scriptures: Proverbs 11:3 and Isaiah 33:15-16

Task: To be honest in all you say and do.

Journal: Record whether or not you were honest in your words and deeds.

Attribute: Love

Scriptures: Luke 6:32-36 and Romans 12:18

Task: To love the unlovely.

Make a list of at least two to five people whom you consider to be difficult to get along with. For this week, make a special effort to extend love and peace toward them. For instance, instead of frowning or dreading when you see them coming your way, smile instead. If they have the tendency to begin an argument, resist the temptation to argue with them. Be prayerful and encouraged!

Journal: Record your experience.

Week 2
Attributes: Joy and Patience

Attribute: Joy

Scriptures: Psalm 126:5-6 and Nehemiah 8:10

Task: To remain joyful in spite of circumstances, and to resist the spirit of discouragement.

Journal: Did you find yourself discouraged any this week? Give an account in your journal.

Attribute: Patience

Scriptures: Galatians 6:9 and Isaiah 40:28-31

Task: To remain patient, and again resist the spirit of discouragement. The process towards an empowering, transformed life is going to require a great amount of patience. Encourage yourself in the scriptures.

Journal: Record your experience.

Week 3
Attributes: Peace and Kindness

Attribute: Peace

Scripture: Philippians 4:6-7

Task: To remain peaceful at *all* times, in good times as well **as bad.**

Journal: Before journaling, read Philippians 4:6-7, and ask yourself, "Did I experience God's kind of peace today?" Record your response.

Attribute: Kindness

Scripture: Ephesians 4:32

Task: To be kind, tenderhearted, and forgiving to others.

Journal: Record your experience.

Week 4
Attributes: Goodness and Faithfulness

Attribute: Goodness

Scripture: Galatians 5:22

Task: To allow the Holy Spirit to operate through you to do what is spiritually and morally fitting always.

Journal: Before you begin your entry, ask yourself, "Today, were my words and deeds pleasing to God? Record your response.

Attribute: Faithfulness

Scripture: Hebrews 11:1,6

Task: To walk by faith.

We have been conditioned to perceive the world we live in through our natural eyes *only*. However, as a child of the **Living** God, in order for you to attain the impossible, you must begin to see the world through your spiritual eyes. For example, writing this workbook was a spiritual journey I embarked upon by faith. I did not have, nor did I know where the finances were going to come from for me to finance this project. However, I knew I was on an assignment from God, and He would see that the work got completed, and He did!

Journal: How did you demonstrate your faith today? Journal your response.

Week 5
Attributes: Gentleness and Self-Control

Attribute: Gentleness

Scripture: Ephesians 4:2

Task: To manifest the commands in the scripture.

Journal: Read the scripture, did you manifest its commands today? Record your response.

Attribute: Self-Control

Scripture: 2 Peter 1:6 and Proverbs 16:32

Task: To control your tongue, temper, and emotions.

Journal: Record your experience.

Lesson VII
Life Success

"They are like trees planted along the riverbanks, bearing fruit each season without fail. Their leaves never wither, and in all they do, they prosper. For the Lord watches over the path of the godly..." Psalm 1:3,6 (LASB)

In this lesson you will be focusing on the **foundational basis** for attaining and living a life of perpetual **success**.

Traditionally, preparation for a life of success primarily focused on life skills training in the areas of employability, money management, and other social skills geared toward preparing an individual in becoming a viable, functioning citizen in his or her community. Training in these areas is very important. This type of training, in addition to the knowledge you will gain from this lesson, will stand you in good stead, you will be well on your way to living a life of perpetual success. Therefore, I strongly recommend you contacting your local county or state job/career service center, or any other agency in your area that offers such training and related services if you are in need of them.

Success

When you think about the word *success* what comes to mind? Webster's New World Dictionary defines success as, "a favorable result," "the gaining of wealth, fame, etc," and "a successful person or thing." The scripture above is consistent with the dictionary's definitions of success. A favorable result is consistent with "*bearing fruit each season **without fail**,*" the gaining of wealth is consistent with "*and **in all** they do **they prosper**,*" and a successful person is consistent with "*the godly*." A life that typifies success is one that is described in Psalm 1:3, 6. It is a godly life that is planted along a life-sustaining source; it bears fruit each season without fail, and it prospers in all it does.

Exercise: In the spaces below write your definition of success and a biblical perspective of success based on Psalm 1:3, 6.

My definition of success is _____

_____

_____

_____

_____

Psalm 1:3,6; Success is _____

_____

_____

The Foundation for a Life of Success

Being anchored to a firm foundation is the only way you are going to live a life of success. As mentioned in the previous lesson, you were blessed with gifts and talents when you were born, and it is through these gifts and talents you will be able to manifest a life of success. However, your gifts and talents **will not** and **cannot** secure you a life of *consistent* and *perpetual* success as mentioned in Psalm 1:3 unless **you** are firmly anchored. The tree in Psalm 1:3 was anchored by its roots. This anchoring is vital; as it will keep you grounded in the **Word** and focused on your purpose. Without an anchor you will utilize your gifts and talents to honor and serve yourself instead of honoring and glorifying God. When this occurs you will find yourself being tossed to and fro as a ship without an anchor on the open seas, and eventually you will self-wreck just as the ship would shipwreck.

So, what is the foundation that you must be anchored to in order for you to have a life of success? It is a foundation that is comprised of the **words** you speak and the **attitude** of your heart.

Words

Words are the most powerful tool you have; they are a gift from God Himself. With mere words, God spoke this world into existence. (Read Genesis 1). There is power in your tongue, and the words you speak **can** and **will** affect your life. "Death and life are in the power of the tongue..." Proverbs 18:21 (NKJV) "And the tongue is a flame of fire. It is full of wickedness that can ruin your whole life. It can turn the entire course of your life into a blazing flame of destruction, for it is set on fire by hell itself." James 3:6 (LASB)

Do you use the power of your words to kill or nourish your life? To answer this question adequately, take a few minutes to think about the words you have spoken to yourself about yourself, your life, your circumstances, and about others around you within the past twenty-four hours. Also, think about the words others have spoken to you that you have agreed with? How many of these words spoken by you and by others were words that nourished life? How many of these words were destructive to life? You may not realize this, but many of the events, and circumstances you have experienced, and maybe experiencing at this time in your life, have been initiated by the words of *others*, and your *very own words*!

In order for you to experience a successful, empowered, transformed life you *must* change your words. With a renewed and fertile mind, this should not be a difficult transition, challenging, yes, but not difficult. Below you will find common situations that you encounter on a daily basis. Read through them and apply the principles to your daily walk.

Exercise:

Common Situations: The book of Proverbs is rich with scriptures about the *tongue* and *words*. The four common situations below are presented with a corresponding scripture (s) and a principle. Memorize the scriptures, or write them down somewhere easily accessible to you. Use the scriptures as a guide to help you apply and incorporate the principles into your daily walk as you encounter each situation. Record your experience in your journal.

Situation #1:	**Daily conversation with others**
Principle:	Practice restraint.
Scripture:	"Don't talk too much, for it fosters sin. Be sensible and turn off the flow!" Proverbs 10:19 (LASB)
Situation #2:	**Fostering relationships**
Principle:	In your relationship with yourself and others use words that nourish, support, encourage, and enhance the relationships.
Scripture:	"Some people make cutting remarks, but the words of the wise bring healing." Proverbs 12:18 (LASB)
Situation #3:	**Hostility**
Principle:	Whenever confronted with hostility practice self-restraint by controlling your tongue.
Scriptures:	"A fool is quick tempered, but a wise person stays calm when insulted." Proverbs 12:16 (LASB)
	"Fools get into constant quarrels; they are asking for a beating. The mouths of fools are their ruin; their lips get them into trouble." Proverbs 18:6-7 (LASB)
	"A gentle answer turns away wrath, but harsh words stir up anger." Proverbs 15:1 (LASB)
	"Those who control their tongue will have a long life; a quick retort can ruin everything." Proverbs 13:3 (LASB)
Situation #4:	**Overcoming everyday temptations and challenges**
Principle:	Remain *forever* encouraged and prayerful.
Scriptures:	"But remember that the temptations that come into your life are no different from what others experience. And God is faithful. He will keep the temptation from becoming so strong that you can't stand up against it. When you are tempted, he will show you a way out so that you will not give in to it. I Corinthians 10:13 (LASB)
	"For God has not given us a spirit of fear, but of power and of love and of a sound mind." 2 Timothy 1:7 (NKJV)

Finally, you have the power within you to change the entire course of your life for the *better* or for the *worst*. As a good steward, it is your responsibility to use your words with discretion and wisdom.

The Attitude of the Heart

"The human heart is most deceitful and desperately wicked. Who really knows how bad it is? But I know! I, the Lord, search all hearts and examine secret motives..." Jeremiah 17:9-10 (LASB)

"For from the heart come evil thoughts, murder, adultery, all other sexual immorality, theft, lying, and slander." Matthew 15:19 (LASB)

Every thought, intention, and emotion is nursed within the bosom of the heart. That is why it is most crucial that you examine the attitude of your heart. According to Jeremiah 17:9, the *human* heart is most deceitful and desperately wicked. After years of being allowed to function in its natural state, the heart eventually becomes hardened. A hardened heart is one that has lost all its *hope*, and its capacity to *care*. A hardened heart is one that has lost *all of its humanity*.

There was a time in my life when I allowed my heart to become even more contaminated by life's venom, and as a result, I developed a hardened heart. My heart attitude was one of hopelessness, self-pity, and despair. In this condition, I resisted the **Father, Son**, and the **Holy Spirit**. With a hardened heart, it is difficult to understand that the only cure for this type of *heart* condition is through Jesus, the Son. Thank God, I came to my senses when I had hit my spiritual bottom. The good thing about hitting bottom is that when I got up, I had to use my knees. I knew I could not go on in the condition I was in. In my desperation, I prayed to God for help, and He healed me. Through prayer and an honest *heartfelt* self-evaluation, I began a daily process of heart attitude examinations.

When was the last time you examined your heart? What is the condition of your heart? What is your heart attitude? Respond to each one of these questions in your journal. If you find that your heart condition and attitude are not what they need to be, STOP! Ask God to heal your heart condition, and give you the right attitude. Everyday evaluate the condition of your heart by asking yourself "What is my heart condition, and the attitude of my heart?" Change what needs to be changed and press on in the Lord.

"...For whatever is in your heart determines what you say." Matthew 12:34 (LASB)

This scripture clearly confirms the connection between the words you speak, and the attitude of your heart. When your heart attitude and words are right, you will have a life of success! Building a life of success based on this foundation will keep you in good stead.

Lesson VIII
Health

I am not talking about health in the physical sense; though, it is most imperative that you maintain good mental and physical health through the care, advice, and recommendations of a physician, or other health care professional. In this lesson you will be focusing on the spiritual benefits you *will* gain by shedding the weight of past hurts and pain, and the heaviness of guilt and shame.

I, like countless others, have experienced hurts, pain, guilt, and shame in the past. Unfortunately, I held onto them, and as a result became heavy laden and unnecessarily overburdened. Are you carrying the weight of past hurts and pain, along with the heaviness of guilt and shame? This type of self-inflicted suffering will hinder your progression, as it did mine for a while towards a transformed, empowered life. Remember, as a steward your responsibility is to glorify God in *all* you do, and living in the past *only* glorifies self.

How do you liberate yourself from the past? Simply by *releasing* it. You have to make a decision today that you are going to free yourself of the weight and heaviness of the past. The **RELEASE** steps below will help you in this process. You will not only shed the weight of past hurts and pain, and the heaviness of guilt and shame, but you will also learn how *not* to put on this type of weight and heaviness ever again.

Releasing IT

Step 1 Receive God's forgiveness and grace.

"If we confess our sins, He is faithful and just to forgive us *our* sins and to cleanse us from all unrighteousness," 1 John1:9 (NKJV)

"I will cleanse away their sins against me, and I will forgive all their sins of rebellion." Jeremiah 33:8 (LASB)

If God, the owner of the life of which you are a steward is willing to forgive you, who are you not to forgive yourself? Receive His forgiveness, then, forgive yourself.

Step 2 Extend genuine apologies to all whom you have wronged. You cannot go back and change the past, it has already occurred; however, you can begin anew. An apology letter is a good new beginning. In your journal, write a letter of apology to all whom you have wronged, be specific. If you feel the need to send the letters to the respective recipients, at some point in time, do so. Do not be discouraged if you find that your apologies are not accepted. You can only do your part.

Step 3 Let others take responsibility for their *own* actions. I learned this the hard way. I carried around the heaviness of guilt and shame for years as a result of being sexually abused by a family member. I felt I was responsible for what had happened to me. I spent countless fruitless hours attempting to make sense of it all. Many years later, I was watching a popular talk show, and a guest on the show said the following words, "let others own their stuff," these words changed my thinking about the situation. These words helped me realize that it was the perpetrator's responsibility to resolve the issue of sexually abusing innocent children. That night, in my journal I wrote a letter to the perpetrator explaining that I was giving him back *his* stuff, it was not mine to have to begin with. At the end of this journal experience, I felt as if a heavy burden had been lifted off of me. Is there a situation where you find yourself burdened with someone else's stuff? ***Give it back to them immediately!*** In your journal write a letter to them.

Step 4   Expecting others to reach out to you with open arms of reciprocity as you go about the business of *releasing* is tantamount to you setting yourself up for a downfall. As stated earlier in step two, you can only do your part. Allow God to do the rest; He can change hearts and minds.

Step 5   Acknowledge and own your stuff. There are some transgressions that are committed against others that transcend egregious. Your actions, good or bad, affect the lives of others. In those instances where your actions have hurt or maybe even destroyed the lives of others directly or indirectly, you must find the courage and strength from deep within to acknowledge and own them. By not acknowledging and owning them, you will be giving the tormenting spirits of *guilt* and *shame* the power to destroy your life. Acknowledge and own your stuff, then, repeat steps *one* and *two.*

Step 6   Seek to forgive. "...and forgive us our sins, just as we have forgiven those who have sinned against us...If you forgive those who sin against you, your heavenly Father will forgive you. But if you refuse to forgive others, your Father will not forgive your sins." Matthew 6:12, 14-15 (LASB)

Forgiving others can be a difficult thing to do. However, if you want God to forgive you for all the wrongs you have done, then, you have to forgive others for all the wrongs they have done to you. At this very moment you are probably thinking, "yeah, right!" Trust me, hating others, and seeking revenge is a waste of good energy and time. It only causes distress. In my struggle to seek to forgive others, I asked the Lord to show me how to do it. He showed me that I was attempting to forgive others in my natural being, and that was *never* going to happen. I had to seek to forgive them from within my *spirit* man, and the Holy Spirit gave me the power to do so through this prayer, "Heavenly Father, help me forgive (blank) for what he/she did. I know I am not capable of forgiving him/her in the natural part of me. Please give me the spirit of forgiveness; I want to be obedient to your word. Thank you Lord. In Jesus' name I pray. Amen."

In your journal you will find several **forgiveness prayers**, insert the names of all those whom you *must* forgive. Remember, forgiving others is a life long daily process. You will know you have forgiven those persons whom you have written a prayer for when you are able to think about them and what they did to you without you becoming agitated and reliving the events.

Step 7 Exonerate yourself. Now is the time for you to make a decision to release yourself from the past. Shed the weight of past hurts and pain, and the heaviness of guilt and shame **forever**. Complete the **Order of Release** below.

Order of Release

"As far as the east is from the west, *So* far has He removed our transgressions from us." Psalm 103:12 (NKJV)

Today (date) _____, I (name) _____ am releasing myself from *all* the weight of past hurts and pain, and the heaviness of guilt and shame. I have served my time. I am determined to be free in my mind, body, and spirit, and begin life **anew**; an empowered, spiritually transformed life! To God be the GLORY!!

Part Three

Lessons 9 to 12

THE SPIRIT

"...I have been crucified with Christ. I myself no longer live, but Christ lives in me. So I live my life in this earthly body by trusting in the Son of God, who loved me and gave himself for me."
Galatians 2:19-20

"As breath is to your physical life, so is your spiritual purpose to the life of your spirit man."

I consider this section of the workbook to be the *most* important. In this section you will (1) identify your spiritual purpose, and (2) understand the importance and significance of your *spiritual* being, your **spirit man**.

In processing the lessons in this section, you will have to adopt a "business" perspective, as this section is presented in such a manner. In part two of this workbook, you learned that you are the steward of the body in which you live. In essence, you are the manager of the *business* of your life. God is the owner.

In most reputable businesses in the natural, you will find four basic constants; one, a mission statement that declares the purpose of the business; two, a delineated and functional structure of the organization; three, standard operating procedures; and four, a system set in place to assess the efficacy of the business' operations and practices, its quality assurance. You will find that these four basic constants hold true for your *business* as well.

- In **lesson nine** you will be declaring your **mission statement** for your business. This is your initial step in establishing your business and declaring your spiritual purpose.
- In **lesson ten** you will discover the **organizational structure** of your business.
- **Lesson eleven** explains how to establish **standard operating procedures** for your business. In this lesson you will also learn the primary duties and responsibilities of your business.
- **Lesson twelve** gives you the opportunity to assess the efficacy of your business' operations and practices, its **quality assurance**.

Lesson IX
Declaring Your Mission Statement

You *cannot* declare a mission statement for your business until you become aware of the nature of your business. Your business is your *life*, and an empowered, transformed life can only exist through a spiritual being, your **"*spirit*"** man. This part of you has probably been completely ignored as you tarried along life's journey; yet, it is the **most** important part of your being. You are first and foremost a *spirit* housed in a physical body. You are created in the image of God, and God is Spirit. Read Genesis 1:27 and John 4:24. It is *only* through your spirit man's relationship with the Father, Son, and Holy Spirit that you are able to *legally* establish your business. Your spirit man's source of empowerment and transformation is derived from its co-existence and relationship with the Father, Son, and Holy Spirit. Therefore, it is most imperative that you acknowledge and understand the importance and the significance of your spirit man's perpetual presence in, and influence over your business.

The first step in establishing your business is to declare your mission statement for your business. This statement must reflect your *spiritual purpose*, the reason or reasons for your business' existence, the services your business provides, and the potential benefits of such provisions. The declaration of your mission statement is most vital to the viability of your business, because every business practice and transaction you will make throughout the life of your business are anchored to it. Simply put, this statement will help guide you and keep you focused on your life's purpose. The following exercise will assist you in declaring your mission statement.

Exercise: Use the worksheet in the journal to create your mission statement, and then write it in the space provided below.

Exercise: Use the worksheet in the journal to create your mission statement, and then write it in the space provided below.

My Mission Statement

_____

_____

_____

_____

_____

_____

_____

_____

_____

_____

Lesson X
Organizational Structure

As a steward, it is most imperative that you have a very clear understanding of the organizational structure within your business. This entails knowing the hierarchical order, and how the chain-of-command flows within the business.

Hierarchical Order

To put is quite succinctly, the hierarchical order simply means, knowing who is in charge. **"...You do not belong to yourself, for God bought you with a high price. So you must honor God with your body." I Corinthians 6:19-20 (LASB)**

Your business is a partnership between you the steward, your spirit man, and the Owner or Chief Executive Officer of your business. The hierarchical order of your business is as follows:

1. At the Head of your business' organizational structure is its actual owner, the triune entity known as the "Trinity." The Trinity is comprised of the **Father, Son, and Holy Spirit**, respectively. The life, strength, and success of any business lie within the Head of the business and the Head's connectedness with the other members of the organization. However, this connectedness has to be one of complete solidarity. Knowing the nature of the Head facilitates this type of connectedness.

The Nature of the Head

The simplest way for me to describe the **Trinity** to you is through the self-wheel that was mentioned in section two of the workbook. Just as one person can be a mom, daughter, and sister, so it is with the Trinity. As one entity, the Trinity functions in three different roles.

Role #1: The Father: The Father is also known as **God**. God is the Father figure of the Trinity, and God is the creator of *all* life. God the Father's nature is first and foremost **love**. See I John 4:8 and John 3:16. God is also **merciful** and **gracious**, Psalms 103:8; God is **forgiving**, Romans 5:15; and God is **faithful**, Numbers 23:19, Joshua 1:9, and Hebrews 13:5.

Role #2: The Son: **Jesus Christ** is the **Son** of God, and his nature is one of **complete submission** and **obedience** to the Father. See Philippians 2:8. It was Jesus, who in *complete* submission and obedience to the Father endured that horrific death on the cross to purchase your life, your *business*, for you. After purchasing your business, His **Father**, who is also your **Father,** placed you as steward over the business.

Role #3: The Holy Spirit: The Holy Spirit, who is also referred to as **The Comforter,** is that part of the Trinity sent by the Father to live within you when

God took Jesus back to heaven. See Luke 24:49. The Holy Spirit is that source that empowers your *spirit man*, thereby facilitating man or woman in becoming all God created him and her to be.

The nature of the Holy Spirit is that of **strength** and **power**. See Romans 8:26-27.

2. The next in line in the hierarchical order of your business is your **spirit man**. As mentioned in the previous lesson, you were created in the image of the Head. The Head is a Spirit (John 4:24), and so are you. When God created your business, He created the business to operate through Him, and the only way to do this is through spiritual means. Therefore, all operations in your business must be conducted on a spiritual basis, through the spirit man's full communion and cooperation with the Head. This communion and cooperation can only be achieved through a personal on-going relationship between the Head and the spirit man.

3. The **Head** cannot and will not commune with the physical or "fleshly" part of your business, the steward, the third and final figure in the hierarchical order. Although the steward assumes this positional order in the hierarchy, this does not diminish its function and responsibilities within the business. In lesson two, you learned that a steward is one who manages another's property. You also leaned that your body is not yours (I Corinthians 6:19-20), it belongs to God, and you are the steward of it. As steward, you have been entrusted to maintain the order and integrity of the business as it apply to the flesh. In short, the steward oversees that the flesh remains subjected to the Spirit. The steward must also realize and oversee the relinquishment of **all** control of business operations to the spirit man. This maintains the legality of the business. The steward **cannot** and **should not** at any time act in the stead of his or her spirit man. A responsible steward who maintains the order and integrity of his or her business will ultimately have a synergistic relationship with his or her spirit man and will not be inclined to take on the role of the spirit man.

Chain-of-Command

Your spirit man needs to have a clear working knowledge of how to navigate itself proficiently and effectively through the chain-of-command within the business' organizational structure. The Head of your business has set in place a simple, but yet profoundly effective system. It is a system that facilitates easy access to the Head in which unobstructed on-going communication takes place, and it is a system that has a clear, delineated description of how the power is distributed throughout the business. This simplistic system will allow for an uncomplicated flow through your business' chain-of-command.

Easy Access to the Head: The Head of your business can be accessed very easily at all times. The **Father,** who is at the top of the hierarchical order and chain-of-command, can always be accessed through His Son, Jesus. Read John 16:23. By using the name of **Jesus**, who is seated at the right hand of the Father (Mark 16:19), your spirit man will be able to converse directly with the Father on a daily basis with boldness through prayer (Hebrews 4:16).

Distribution of Power: As the Head *is* the Chief Executive Officer and Owner of the business, He secures the highest position of authority and ultimate power in the business. He also has *total* control of the business. With that being said, all, and I mean **all** business transactions and decisions must go through Him. See Matthew 6:33 and Proverbs 3:5-6. The Head has also empowered your spirit man with the indwelling of the Holy Spirit, See John 14:15-18. Because of this, your spirit man has the authority and power to cancel all attacks, schemes, and devises of the enemy that are designed to abort your spiritual purpose and ultimately your business (Luke 10:19). Finally, power has also been given to angels who are administrative assistants in your business. Their assignment is to assist in the day-to-day business operations. See Hebrews 1:14.

So you see the **Head** has set in place a well organized system for you to conduct your *business* within. These plans were set in place from the time you were created. "For I know the plans I have for you," says the Lord. "They are plans for good and not for disaster, to give you a future and a hope." Jeremiah 29:11 (LASB)

Complete the following exercise by filling in the blanks.

1. Your *"business"* is your _____, and it is a partnership between you the _____, your spirit _____, and the _____.

2. The owner, CEO, or Head of your business is the Trinity; the Trinity is comprised of the _____, _____, and the _____ _____.

3. The life, strength, and success of your business lie in the _____ _____ between the Head, your spirit man, and you the steward.

4. The nature of the **Father/God** is first and foremost _____. He is also _____, _____, _____, and __ _____. The nature of the **Son, Jesus Christ** is that of complete _____ and _____. The **Holy Spirit's** nature is that of _____ and _____.

5. Your business was purchased by Jesus, and the Father placed you as _____ _____ _____ over it.

6. The next in line after the Trinity in the hierarchical order is your _____
_____.

7. When God created your business He created it to operate through Him. How is the Head able to operate through your business? _____
_____
_____
_____
_____

8. Why is it *not* possible for the steward to stand in the stead of your spirit man at any time? _____
_____
_____
_____

9. What makes the flow through the chain-of-command in your business an uncomplicated one? _____
_____
_____
_____

10. How easy is it to access the **Head** of your business? What scriptures support your answer?
_____
_____
_____
_____

11. How is the power distributed along the chain-of-command in your business?
_____
_____
_____
_____
_____

12. In your journal draw *detailed* pictorials of the **hierarchical order** and the **chain-of-command** in your business. Using arrows indicate the flow of communication in the chain-of-command, and the flow of power in the hierarchy. Include brief descriptions of all the members involved in the hierarchy and chain-of-command, and brief descriptions about how both systems function.

Lesson XI
Standard Operating Procedures

In order for your business to honor the commitment set forth in its mission statement, and function proficiently on a day-to-day basis in accomplishing its primary duties and responsibilities, there *must* be an established code of conduct, or a system of rules and procedures in place by which **all** business operations are based upon. This code of conduct or system of rules and procedures are generally established through a method known as *standard operating procedures*.

Before standard operating procedures for your business are established, you, the steward, must be aware of the two antithetical forces embedded within the *heart* of your business. These two forces, the **sinful** nature and the **Spiritual** nature, are constantly at war vying for control of your business. It is most imperative that you familiarize yourself with the nature of the two forces, as one force will maintain your business' purpose and integrity, while the other will *completely* destroy your business.

"The old sinful nature loves to do evil, which is just opposite from what the Holy Spirit wants. And the Spirit gives us desires that are opposite from what the sinful nature desires. These two forces are constantly fighting each other, and your choices are never free from this conflict." Galatians 5:17 (LASB)

Force I

The Sinful Nature

You are quite familiar with the sinful nature. It is that part of your being that tells you to do as you please regardless of others' feelings, or inconveniences. It is that part of your being that is self-absorbed, selfish, and self-destructive! The sinful nature **is out of order and control**! When left to its own vices, the sinful nature will produce perpetual chaos and lawlessness such as sexual immorality, impure thoughts, eagerness for lustful pleasure, idolatry, participation in demonic activities, hostility, quarreling, jealousy, outburst of anger, selfish ambition, divisions, the feeling that everyone is wrong except those in your own little group, envy, murder, drunkenness, wild parties, and other kinds of sin. Galatians 5:19-21 (LASB).

How is it that mankind seems to be powerless to the forces of this nature? Because man was born in iniquity, and it just seems natural to indulge the flesh in its filth. (See Psalms 51:5) However, if the sinful nature is allowed any position of authority or influence in your business, the end result will be *spiritual death* and the demise of your business.

Force II

The Spiritual Nature

The Spiritual nature is the Holy Spirit. In the previous lesson you learned that the Holy Spirit's nature is that of strength and empowerment, and that the Holy Spirit lives within you.

The fact that you were born in iniquity is *no* longer an issue once you allow the Holy Spirit to take control. Because the Holy Spirit lives within you through your spirit man, you are at liberty to live a Spirit-filled, Spirit-led powerful life free from the bondage of sin and fleshly desires. As a result of this freedom, your business will produce the fruits of love, joy, peace, patience, kindness, goodness, faithfulness, gentleness, and self-control, **all** of which spell *success*. Galatians 5:22-23 (LASB)

Establishing Your Standard Operating Procedures

In establishing the standard operating procedures for your business, there are *three* fundamental truths that the steward, in conjunction with the spirit man need to build them upon.

- **Truth #1.** *Submit everything in your business to God.* What are the benefits of this? When trouble and persecution come against your business as a result of a spiritual attack from the enemy, you will be able to resist the enemy, and the enemy will have to flee from you. See James 4:7

- **Truth #2.** *Let Jesus tame the beast (the sinful nature) within.* Read Paul's account in Romans 7:14-24. Paul talked about desiring and agreeing to do what was right, but ultimately ended up doing the opposite because of his sinful nature. He concluded by saying only Jesus Christ was able to free him from a life that was dominated by sin. Jesus Christ tamed Paul's beast within, He can do the same for you. Let Him!

- **Truth #3.** *Realize the guaranteed victory given to you by God.* When you encounter **any** temptation which will violate your business' standards and compromise its integrity, remember you are guaranteed the victory in these circumstances. "But remember that the temptations that come into your life are no different from what others experience. **And God is faithful**. He will keep the temptation from becoming so strong that you can't stand up against it. When you are tempted, he will show you a way out so that you will not give in to it." I Corinthians 10:13 (LASB, emphasis added)

If you noticed, all of these truths are connected to the **Head** of your business. God, the Father will allow you to stand up victoriously against the enemy as long as you are submitted to Him. The Son, Jesus will tame the sinful nature; thereby, providing you with more power and victory in your business. Finally, because God is faithful toward the success of your business, He empowers you with the Holy Spirit who helps you escape from the strongholds of temptations.

Henceforth, the success of your business is directly related to the following principles; *self-discipline, avoiding temptations, obedience and submission to the Head, and the outward manifestations of the fruits of the Spirit.* By establishing standard operating procedures based upon the three fundamental truths for these principles, you will secure a spiritually sound system that is bound to yield optimal order and success for your business. For instance, there are going to be times when practicing self-discipline will prove to be *extremely* challenging, and you may find yourself in a situation that has the potential to compromise the business' integrity, or even destroy the business. By being able to refer to and employ the procedures you have set in place for practicing self-discipline, you will be able to overcome the temptation to give in to the flesh and make poor decisions.

Journal Exercise: Using the three fundamental truths, in your journal *create* Standard Operating Procedures for the principles below. You have already explored some of these principles in the Character Building Exercise in part two of the workbook.

1. Demonstrating and practicing self discipline
2. Avoiding temptations
3. Being obedient and submissive to the Head
4. Demonstrating and practicing qualities such as righteousness, holiness, integrity, commitment, loyalty, perseverance, faith, hope, and love-----**outward manifestation of the fruits of the Spirit.**

Duties and Responsibilities

In your business, your primary duties and responsibilities lie within three main service areas. These service areas are that of **worship**, **love,** and **witnessing**, respectively. In order for you to execute your duties and responsibilities effectively and proficiently, you will need three essential invaluable resources in addition to the standard operating procedures. As a prudent steward, it is your responsibility to avail yourself of these necessary resources.

The *most* invaluable resource that is readily available to you is your **Bible**; *it is your training manual.* Another invaluable resource is a *good* Bible teaching, *Christ*-centered church. A church that is led by a pastor of integrity, and one who ministers to the "*whole"* being. Lastly, having a few spirit-led men and women of God as mentors and companions are other invaluable resources.

Worship

As mentioned earlier, there must be an established on-going relationship between your spirit man and the Head. To get the *full* attention of God the Father is to *worship* Him, and this can only be done through a relationship. When you worship God, you are acknowledging and honoring His Lordship over your business. You are to worship God daily. Just by saying, "God I adore you," "I love you," "I thank you for being my Lord and Savior", "You are worthy of all my praises," *is* worshipping God. Worshipping God is a privilege that should be cherished and *never* forsaken, *nor* taken for granted.

"Oh come, let us worship and bow down; Let us kneel before the Lord our Maker..."
Psalm 95:6 (LASB)

Love

"And you must love the Lord your God with all your heart, all your soul, and all your strength." Deuteronomy 6:5 (LASB)

The service area of love is twofold: the love for God, and the love for others. The Word of God declares you are a liar if you say you love God whom you have not seen, but hate your Christian brothers and sisters whom you have seen. (See I John 4:20) Loving others is a commandment from the Lord. By loving others you will demonstrate your love for God, which will yield great profit in your business. (See I Corinthians 13) Remember, God is not going to command you to do something without giving you the grace to accomplish it.

"So now I am giving you a new commandment: Love each other. Just as I have loved you, you should love each other. Your love for one another will prove to the world that you are my disciples," John 13:34-35 (LASB)

Witnessing

You are responsible for spreading the Good News about the Kingdom of God to others. You do this by witnessing or telling others about the goodness of God and His free gift of *salvation*. Your life can also be a witness. By living a life that is holy and righteousness before God and man, you will be witnessing to others. They will see the difference in you, and be drawn to you by the peace of God that emanates from you, and by the light of God that shines through you.

"God sent John the Baptist to tell everyone about the light so that everyone might believe because of his testimony. John himself was not the light; he was only a ***witness*** to the light." John 1: 6-8 (LASB, emphasis added)

Exercise: In your journal describe how you plan on fulfilling your duties and responsibilities in the services areas of worship, love, and witnessing.

Lesson XII
Quality Assurance

"Yes, each of us will have to give a personal account to God." Romans 14:12 (LASB)

Many businesses in the natural are ruined due to a lack of accountability, and so it will be for your *business* if you do not incorporate a system of accountability into your business' practices. Without accountability, qualities such as righteousness, holiness, discretion, integrity, commitment, loyalty, perseverance, faith, hope, and love will become unimportant and insignificant. Without such qualities, your business *will* perish. The accountability evaluation below will assist you in monitoring how well your business is functioning. I strongly recommended you use this assessment tool *regularly* throughout the life of your business.

Accountability Evaluation

Place a check in the appropriate spaces.

A. Mission Statement

1. Are the purpose(s) and objectives of the mission statement being met? Explain.

_____

_____

_____

_____

_____

_____

B. Organizational Structure

2. The connectedness between the Head, spirit man, and steward is

( ) Extremely strong   ( ) Very strong ( ) Somewhat strong
( ) Not strong at all.

Explain: _____

_____

_____

_____

_____

3. The relationship that exists between the spirit man and the Head is

( ) Extremely close ( ) Very close ( ) Somewhat close ( ) Not close at all

Explain: _____

_____

_____

_____

4. The relationship that exists between the steward and the spirit man is
( ) Extremely close ( ) Very close ( ) Somewhat close ( ) Not close at all
Explain: _____

_____

_____

_____

5. As steward, I relinquish **all** control of my business operations to my spirit man
( ) All of the time ( ) Most of the time ( ) Some of the time
( ) None of the time
Explain: _____

_____

_____

_____

_____

_____

6. My spirit man understands and navigates through my business' chain-of-
command with profound efficacy and precision
( ) All of the time ( ) Most of the time ( ) Some of the time
( ) None of the time

B. Standard Operating Procedures

7. On a daily basis, I am able to resist the enemy (satan), because I submit
everything about my business to the Lord
( ) All the time ( ) Most of the time ( ) Some of the time
( ) None of the time
Explain: _____

_____

_____

_____

8. On a daily basis, I allow the Head to take control of the beast
(sinful nature) within
( ) All the time ( ) Most of the time ( ) Some of the time
( ) None of the time
Explain: _____

_____

_____

_____

9. On a daily basis, I have victory over temptations because I
am able to recognize and employ the way out of the temptations provided for me
   by the Head
(   ) All of the time (   ) Most of the time (   ) Some of the time
(   ) None of the time

Explain: _____

_____

_____

_____

10. The Standard Operating Procedures I have established for my business are
   effective
(   ) All of the time (   ) Most of the time (   ) Some of the time
(   ) None of the time
Explain: _____

_____

_____

_____

C. Duties and Responsibilities

11. In performing my duties and responsibilities in the service
areas of worship, love, and witnessing, **I**
 a. use my training manual, **The Holy Bible**
(   ) All the time (   ) Most of the time (   ) Some of the time
(   ) None of the time
Explain: _____

_____

_____

_____

b. attend a Bible-teaching, Christ-centered church
(   ) All the time (   ) Most of the time (   ) Some of the time
(   ) None of the time
Explain: _____

_____

_____

_____

c. have cultivated the friendship and mentoring of a few spirit-
led and spirit-filled brothers and sisters in Christ. Write their
names in the space provided.

My brothers and sisters in Christ are _____

_____

_____

_____

_____

_____

_____

_____

_____

12. In honoring my duties and responsibilities in the service area of **worship**, I rate

(   ) Extremely high (   ) Very high (   ) Somewhat high (   ) Not high at all

Explain: _____

_____

_____

_____

_____

13. In honoring my duties and responsibilities in the service area of **love**, I rate

(   ) Extremely high (   ) Very high (   ) Somewhat high (   ) Not high at all

Explain: _____

_____

_____

_____

_____

14. In honoring my duties and responsibilities in the service area of **witnessing**, I rate

(   ) Extremely high (   ) Very high (   ) Somewhat high (   ) Not high at all

Explain: _____

_____

_____

_____

_____

D. Recommendations

After completing the evaluation, take a few minutes and reflect upon your responses.

Identify your areas of strengths and weaknesses. What adjustments and/or recommendation(s) for improvement would you make in your weak areas? How are you going to maintain your areas of strength?

Explain: _____

_____

_____

_____

_____

_____

_____

_____

_____

_____

_____

_____

_____

_____

_____

_____

_____

_____

_____

_____

_____

_____

_____

_____

_____

_____

_____

_____

_____

Conclusion

Congratulations! You have completed all the exercises in this workbook. However, your journey continues, remember you are a work in progress. I trust and pray that you continue to allow the Holy Spirit the opportunity to transform you into the spiritually empowered man or woman God created you to be. See Philippians 1:6 Now, you have one more task to complete, answer the following question:

What type of harvest have you yielded from your garden of H.O.P.E thus far?

_____

_____

_____

_____

_____

_____

_____

_____

It may take some of your seeds of expectation a little longer to yield the harvest you hoped for, do not grow weary; remember, seeds that are sown in good soil *will* produce a bountiful harvest. Keep the faith, remain encouraged and hopeful, and in due season you will have all that the Lord has in store for you. He did it for me and He will certainly do it for you, because He **does not** show favoritism. Acts 10:34

ENDNOTES

Part One

1. Life Application Study Bible, Dictionary/Concordance (Wheaton, IL: Tyndale House Publishers, 1996), 2204

2. Life Application Study Bible, Dictionary/Concordance (Wheaton, IL: Tyndale House Publishers, 1996), 2197

GARDEN OF H.O.P.E.

Holding Onto Positive Expectations

Garden of H.O.P.E.

H.O.P.E.

Holding Onto Positive Expectations

A Spiritual Journey Towards An Empowering
Transformed Life

Journal

Introduction
Refection Notes

_____

_____

_____

_____

_____

_____

_____

_____

_____

_____

_____

_____

_____

_____

_____

_____

_____

_____

_____

_____

_____

_____

_____

Part One

Lessons 1 to 4

THE MIND

"…But we can understand these things, for we have the mind of Christ."
1 Corinthians 2:16

Lesson I
Reflection Notes

Lesson II

Tilling the Soil: Plowing and Harrowing
Journal Exercise

Step II

Harrowing

For each item you placed a **(X)** next to in the plowing exercise briefly describe each one, and provide an account about what occurred as you harrowed your mind soil.

Non-Productive Thoughts:

_____
_____
_____
_____
_____
_____
_____
_____
_____

Negative Thinking:

_____
_____
_____
_____
_____
_____
_____

Friends and Associates:

_____
_____
_____
_____
_____
_____

Unhealthy Relationships:

Destructive Behaviors:

Family Members:

Tradition:

_____

_____

_____

_____

_____

_____

_____

Lesson II
Reflection Notes

Lesson III

Tilling the Soil: Fertilization

Journal Exercise

Planting Your Seeds of Expectation

You have completed the work of tilling, congratulations! You are ready to plant your *seeds of expectation*; your mind is now fertile, productive ground for you to plant in, with the ability to return a **one hundredfold** harvest. Review your list of seeds of expectation again, and prayerfully ask the Holy Spirit to guide you in planting *only* the seeds that are in His will for your renewed transformed life. **Read Psalm 37:4-5**

In the space below draw your garden of H.O.P.E., and plant your seeds of expectation.

Lesson III
Reflection Notes

Lesson IV

Tending the Garden
Journal Exercise
"How Well Are You Tending Your Garden?"

Over the next eight weeks, tend to your garden, and record your progress weekly on the schedules. *Always* seek the wisdom and guidance of the Holy Spirit before you begin your daily entries.

A **"PW"** indicates you are progressing well. That is, you are providing the adequate amount of water to your plants, you continue to fertilize the soil, there are no weeds growing in your garden, and you are definitely safeguarding against trespassers.

An upper case **"W"** indicates *too much* water; a lower case **"w"** indicates *too little* water. A smiley face :) indicates that the adequate amount of water is being applied to your garden. Whenever you pull a weed from your garden, indicate this by *naming* the type of weed you pulled. An **"O"** indicates you are being influenced negatively by other people's opinion(s).

Each day write a reflective entry about your progress. Even if you have experienced a "PW" type of day, describe the events that occurred in that day to make it a good day. If you find you are overly excited and/or anxious, fearful, or doubtful, explore the reason/s for these emotions. On the days you pulled a weed or two, explore how you allowed that particular weed to invade your garden. Whenever you discover your efforts are being thwarted by the opinions of others, seek to understand why you have allowed their opinions to have control over you.

This type of on-going evaluation will assist you in becoming aware of the dynamics within, as well as around you; thereby, enabling you with the ability to secure and maintain the integrity of your garden with much confidence. It is also an indication of your spiritual maturation.

This type of on-going evaluation will assist you in becoming aware of the dynamics within, as well as around you; thereby, enabling you with the ability to secure and maintain the integrity of your garden with much confidence. It is also an indication of your spiritual maturation.

Week 1

Days	1	2	3	4	5	6	7
Activity							
Water							
Weed							
Fertilize							
Safeguarding							

Reflection Notes

_____

_____

_____

_____

_____

_____

_____

_____

_____

Week 2

Days	1	2	3	4	5	6	7
Activity							
Water							
Weed							
Fertilize							
Safeguarding							

Reflection Notes

_____

_____

_____

_____

_____

_____

_____

_____

_____

_____

_____

Week 3

Days	1	2	3	4	5	6	7
Activity							
Water							
Weed							
Fertilize							
Safeguarding							

Reflection Notes

_____

_____

_____

_____
_____
_____
_____
_____
_____
_____

Week 4

Days	1	2	3	4	5	6	7
Activity							
Water							
Weed							
Fertilize							
Safeguarding							

Reflection Notes

_____
_____
_____
_____
_____
_____
_____
_____
_____
_____

Week 5

Days	1	2	3	4	5	6	7
Activity							
Water							
Weed							
Fertilize							
Safeguarding							

Reflection Notes

_____

_____

_____

_____

_____

_____

_____

_____

_____

_____

Week 6

Days	1	2	3	4	5	6	7
Activity							
Water							
Weed							
Fertilize							
Safeguarding							

Reflection Notes

_____
_____
_____
_____
_____
_____
_____
_____
_____
_____

Week 7

Days	1	2	3	4	5	6	7
Activity							
Water							
Weed							
Fertilize							
Safeguarding							

Reflection Notes

_____
_____
_____
_____
_____
_____
_____
_____
_____

Week 8

Days	1	2	3	4	5	6	7
Activity							
Water							
Weed							
Fertilize							
Safeguarding							

Reflection Notes

_____

_____

_____

_____

_____

_____

_____

_____

_____

Lesson IV
Reflection Notes

Part Two

Lessons 5 to 8

THE BODY

"You made all the delicate, inner parts of my body and knit me together in my mother's womb. Thank you for making me so wonderfully complex! Your workmanship is marvelous…"
Psalm 139:13-14

Lesson V

Relationships

*Role: _____

Expectations and Demands: _____

_____

_____

_____

*Role: _____

Expectations and Demands: _____

_____

_____

_____

*Role: _____

Expectations and Demands: _____

_____

_____

_____

*Role: _____

Expectations and Demands: _____

_____

_____

_____

Part II. "True" Self Essay
Complete the following essay:

The other day as I was walking, I saw someone who looked quite familiar. As I got closer to the person, I realized that it was me, not the me I used to be, but the me I became when I decided to walk into my "true' self. I knew it was my true self because _____

_____

_____

_____

_____

_____

_____

_____

_____

_____

_____

_____

_____

_____

_____

_____

_____

_____

_____

_____

_____

_____

_____

_____

_____

_____

_____

_____

_____

_____

_____

Lesson V
Reflection Notes

Lesson VI

Personal Growth
Actualization of Gifts and Talents

It is most imperative that you complete a plan of action for the development and actualization of your gifts and talents. For instance, a person may be a natural or have a superior ability in computer skills, but lack the formal education and certification needed to enter into doors that should readily be open to him or her. In order for this person to succeed in this area, he or she must first receive the education and certification needed. Yes, the Lord *did* bless this person with this ability, but is he or she being a good steward? A good steward will do what is needed to maximize to its full potential all of his or her gifts and/or talents.

On the other hand, a person may have formal training in the area of his or her gifting and talent, but is not manifesting his or her full potential in the areas of his or her gifting and talents. In many cases like this, the flesh is being honored and glorified instead of God.

Exercise: On the next two pages write your plan of action for the development and actualization of your gifts and talents. If this involves going back to school or receiving further training, write a detailed account about what school you plan on attending, or what training you plan on receiving, when do you plan on beginning, the length of your schooling or training, your financial resources, etc. Also, include in your plan, how you are going to honor and glorify God with your gifts and talents.

My Complete Plan of Action for the Development and Actualization of My Gifts and Talents

My Complete Plan of Action for the Development and Actualization of My Gifts and Talents

_____
_____
_____
_____
_____
_____
_____
_____
_____
_____
_____
_____
_____
_____
_____
_____
_____
_____
_____
_____
_____
_____
_____
_____
_____
_____
_____
_____

Character Building
Week 1
Attributes: Integrity and Love

Sunday _____
_____
_____
_____
_____

Monday _____
_____
_____
_____
_____

Tuesday _____
_____
_____
_____
_____

Wednesday _____
_____
_____
_____
_____

Thursday _____
_____
_____
_____
_____

Friday _____
_____
_____

Saturday _____

_____

_____

_____

_____

Week 2
Attributes: Joy and Patience

Sunday _____

_____

_____

_____

Monday _____

_____

_____

_____

_____

Tuesday _____

_____

_____

_____

Wednesday _____

_____

_____

_____

Thursday _____

_____
_____
_____

Friday _____
_____
_____
_____

Saturday _____
_____
_____
_____

Week 3
Attributes: Peace and Kindness

Sunday _____
_____
_____
_____

Monday _____
_____
_____
_____

Tuesday _____
_____
_____
_____

Wednesday _____

_____

_____

_____

Thursday _____

_____

_____

_____

Friday _____

_____

_____

_____

_____

Saturday _____

_____

_____

_____

_____

Week 4
Attributes: Goodness and Faithfulness

Sunday _____

_____

_____

_____

_____

Monday _____

_____

_____

_____

_____

Tuesday _____

_____

_____

_____

Wednesday _____

_____

_____

_____

Thursday _____

_____

_____

_____

Friday _____

_____

_____

_____

Saturday _____

_____

_____

_____

_____

Week 5
Attributes: Gentleness and Self-Control

Sunday _____

_____

_____

_____

Monday _____

_____

_____

_____

Tuesday _____

_____

_____

_____

Wednesday _____

_____

_____

_____

Thursday _____

_____

_____

_____

Friday _____

_____

_____

_____

Saturday _____

_____

_____

_____

_____

Lesson VI
Reflection Notes

Week VII

Life Success
Words

You were given principles to live by for four **common situations** that you may encounter on a daily basis. In the spaces below recall how you applied each principle. Begin by first describing the situation, and secondly, your response.

Situation #1: Daily conversation with others.

_____

_____

_____

_____

_____

Situation #2: Fostering relationships.

_____

_____

_____

_____

_____

Situation #3: Hostility

_____

_____

_____

_____

Situation #4: Overcoming everyday temptations and challenges.

_____

_____

_____

_____

_____

Lesson VII

Life Success

The Attitude of the Heart

"The human heart is most deceitful and desperately wicked. Who really knows how bad it is? But I know! I, the Lord, search all hearts and examine secret motives..." Jeremiah 17:19-10 (LASB)

Exercise: Complete the following questions:

1. When was the last time you examined your heart? _____
_____
_____
_____
_____
_____

2. What is the condition of your heart? _____
_____
_____
_____
_____

3. What is your heart attitude? _____
_____
_____
_____
_____

Lesson VII
Reflection Notes

Lesson VIII

Health
Releasing IT

Step 2: Letters of Apology

Letter #1

_____

_____

_____

_____

_____

_____

_____

_____

_____

_____

_____

_____

_____

_____

_____

_____

_____

Letter #2

_____

_____

_____

_____

_____

Letter #3

_____

_____

_____

_____

_____

_____

_____

_____

_____

_____

Letter #4

_____

_____

_____

_____

_____

_____

_____

_____

_____

_____

_____

_____

_____

_____

_____

_____

_____

_____

Letter #5

Step 3: "Let others own *their* stuff" letters.

Letter #1

_____

_____

_____

_____

_____

_____

_____

_____

_____

_____

_____

_____

_____

_____

_____

_____

_____

_____

_____

_____

_____

Letter #2

_____

_____

_____

_____

_____

_____

_____

Letter #3

Letter #4

Letter #5

Step 6: Prayer of Forgiving

"Heavenly Father, help me forgive (_____) for what he/she did. I know I am not capable of forgiving him/her in the natural part of me. Please give me the spirit of forgiveness; I want to be obedient to your word. Thank you Lord. In Jesus' name I pray. Amen"

"Heavenly Father, help me forgive (_____) for what he/she did. I know I am not capable of forgiving him/her in the natural part of me. Please give me the spirit of forgiveness; I want to be obedient to your word. Thank you Lord. In Jesus' name I pray. Amen"

"Heavenly Father, help me forgive (_____) for what he/she did. I know I am not capable of forgiving him/her in the natural part of me. Please give me the spirit of forgiveness; I want to be obedient to your word. Thank you Lord. In Jesus' name I pray. Amen"

"Heavenly Father, help me forgive (_____) for what he/she did. I know I am not capable of forgiving him/her in the natural part of me. Please give me the spirit of forgiveness; I want to be obedient to your word. Thank you Lord. In Jesus' name I pray. Amen"

"Heavenly Father, help me forgive (_____) for what he/she did. I know I am not capable of forgiving him/her in the natural part of me. Please give me the spirit of forgiveness; I want to be obedient to your word. Thank you Lord. In Jesus' name I pray. Amen"

"Heavenly Father, help me forgive (_____) for what he/she did. I know I am not capable of forgiving him/her in the natural part of me. Please give me the spirit of forgiveness; I want to be obedient to your word. Thank you Lord. In Jesus' name I pray. Amen"

Lesson VIII
Reflection Notes

_____

_____

_____

_____

_____

_____

_____

_____

_____

_____

_____

_____

_____

_____

_____

_____

_____

_____

_____

_____

_____

_____

_____

_____

_____

Part Three

Lessons 9 to 12

THE SPIRIT

"…I have been crucified with Christ. I myself no longer live, but Christ lives in me. So I live my life in this earthly body by trusting in the Son of God, who loved me and gave himself for me."
Galatians 2:19-20

Lesson IX

Declaring Your Mission Statement
Worksheet

"Now My soul is troubled, and what shall I say? Father, save Me from this hour? But for this ***purpose*** I came to this hour. Father, glorify Your name." John 12:27-28 (NJKV, emphasis added)

These were the words of **Jesus**. He was expressing His feelings about His impending sacrificial death, which was coming to earth in the form of man, and unselfishly dying on a cross like a common criminal for your sins and mine. I think this scripture is most fitting to use as a guide to help you create your mission statement for your *business*.

- "...But for this purpose I came to this hour..." What was Jesus' **spiritual purpose**? To die on a cross for **our** sins.
- What was Jesus' **reason(s) for existing**? **(See John 3:16-17, and John 14:6)**
- What **services** did Jesus provide, and what were the **benefits** of such provision? **"...Father, glorify Your name..."** First, He demonstrated to mankind how to glorify the name of the Father through HIS *absolute* obedience and submission to the Father; and secondly, He provided mankind an escape from eternal death by providing the **Way** for us to have eternal life through HIS *unconditional and utmost expression of love and sacrifice.* His provision benefited us by giving us life eternal through salvation, and a life of abundance. Read John 10:10
- If Jesus were to write a mission statement when He was here on earth, I believe it would read like this:

Jesus' Mission Statement: To suffer a sacrificial death upon a cross for mankind. This unconditional and utmost expression of love will glorify the Father, and provide humanity **The Way** out of eternal death into an abundant and *eternal* life through salvation.

Worksheet

Exercise: Using the provided guide, create your mission statement for your *business* by completing the questions below.

1. What is your spiritual purpose? If you do not know, ask the Holy Spirit to reveal it to you. Your spiritual purpose will be connected to your gifts/talents, and ***always*** consistent with Kingdom business.

   _____

   _____

   _____

2. What is/are the reason(s) for the existence of your *business*? Remember, your *business* is your life.

   _____

   _____

   _____

3. What service does your business provide, and how are they beneficial to others?

   _____

   _____

   _____

4. Now put all of your responses together and write a simple statement that reflects your spiritual purpose, the reason (s) for your business' existence, the services your business provides, and the benefits of your services. This will be your ***mission statement***. Re-write the statement in the space provided in your workbook.

   _____

   _____

   _____

   _____

   _____

Lesson IX
Reflection Notes

Lesson X

Organizational Structure

Exercise: Draw *detailed* pictorials of the *hierarchical order* and the *chain-of-command* in your business. Using arrows indicate the flow of communication in the chain-of-command, and the flow of power in the hierarchy. Include brief descriptions of all the members involved the hierarchy and chain-of-command, and brief descriptions about how both systems function.

Hierarchical Order

Chain-of-Command

Lesson X
Reflection Notes

Lesson XI

Standard Operating Procedures

Exercise: Complete **standard operating procedures**, that is, the way you intend on *functioning* and *performing* on a daily and consistent basis in the following areas:

A. Demonstrating and practicing self-discipline: _____

_____

_____

_____

_____

_____

B. Avoiding temptations: _____

_____

_____

_____

_____

_____

C. Being obedient and submissive to Head: _____

_____

_____

_____

_____

_____

D. Demonstrating and practicing qualities such as righteousness, holiness, integrity, commitment, loyalty, perseverance, faith, hope, and love.

      1. Righteousness _____

_____

_____

_____

      2. Holiness _____

_____

_____

_____

3. Integrity _____
_____
_____
_____

4. Commitment _____
_____
_____
_____

5. Loyalty _____
_____
_____
_____

6. Perseverance _____
_____
_____
_____

7. Faith _____
_____
_____
_____

8. Hope _____
_____
_____
_____

9. Love _____
_____
_____
_____

Andrea J. Williams M.S.

Lesson XI

Standard Operating Procedures

Exercise: In the spaces below, provide a detailed account of how you plan on fulfilling your duties and responsibilities in the service areas of worship, love, and witnessing.

Worship: _____

_____

_____

_____

_____

_____

_____

Love: _____

_____

_____

_____

_____

_____

_____

Witnessing: _____

_____

_____

_____

_____

_____

Lesson XI
Reflection Notes

Lesson XII

Quality Assurance

Reflection Notes

Conclusion
Reflection Notes

About the Author

I was born and raised in Nassau Bahamas. In the mid 1980's I traveled to the United States to pursue a college education. Married for twenty-three years, my husband and I have two children and one grandson.

In June 2001, I went to work at a correctional facility as an instructor teaching parenting, life skills, and anger management classes to the inmate population. I was unaware of the *tremendous* spiritual impact this employment opportunity would have upon my life.

Working with the inmate population was very rewarding; however, I felt compelled to broaden my horizons with the gift I have for teaching and encouraging others. This curriculum/workbook is the product of that compulsion. In the capacity of a Spiritual Life Coach, it is my heart's desire to continue empowering others spiritually.